all the *way*

SEX FOR THE FIRST TIME

SEX FOR THE FIRST TIME

by Kim Martyn

National Library Of Canada Cataloguing In Publication Data

Martyn Kim
All the way: sex for the first time/Kim Martyn.

Includes bibliographical references and index.
ISBN 1-894549-26-0

1. Sex instruction for teenagers. I. Title.

HQ27.M37 2003 613.9'51 C2003-903739-8

Second printing 2007

Edited by Rhea Tregebov
Cover illustration by Kim Smith
Design by Elizabeth Martin

Sumach Press acknowledges the support of the Canada Council for the Arts and the Ontario Arts Council for our publishing program. We acknowledge the Government of Ontario through the Ontario Media Development Corporation's Ontario Book Initiative.

Printed and bound in Canada

Published by

SUMACH PRESS
1415 Bathurst Street #202
Toronto Canada
M5R 3H8

sumachpress@on.aibn.com

www.sumachpress.com

This book is dedicated to Bruce, Kendra and Emma

ACKNOWLEDGEMENTS

A huge thanks to all those people who've made this project possible. Chronologically, to my mom for her quiet unfaltering support. To my dad for his determination to raise Rob, Steve and me in a more sexually positive and open way. To Susan and Theresa for our early games and later wisdom. To Sue for training me in the first place and Jane for listening and laughing. To my sweet Bruce, who had a vision of me doing this before I did and helped me stay focused. And Kendra and Emma, who've put up all their life with a mom who's always talkin' about sex stuff! To Liz, Isobel and Bruce for the ways you stand behind me. To my amazing colleagues at Toronto Public Health, especially Lyba, Ruth and Ann, for keeping me on my toes!

To all of you who graciously shared your "first time" and early experience stories with me — thanks … your anonymity is safe!

I could not have moved forward without the thumbs up from my youth readers: Camilla Colter, David Laing, Miranda Morningstar and Tom Buchanan.

And a special thanks to the fabulous women at Sumach Press: Beth, Jamila, Liz, Lois, Noelle and Rhea. I could not have dreamed up a better team to work with. They have been so enthusiastic, encouraging and creative in their suggestions, all the while working their butts off.

Finally — a humble acknowledgement of the trees used in making these many pages … may we find a way to make such things out of garbage sooner than later.

Contents

introduction

You've been making out forever. HOT, TASTY AND SWEET. Kissing, rubbing and maybe sometimes coming. Not, however, being entered or entering. No "sex." Not doing it. Not yet. And now you think you might be ready to go there. ***First time.*** ALL THE WAY.

You may wonder, *what's all that hot stuff we've been doing?* Sex, of course!! But not intercourse. Doing it, the wild thing, making love, getting laid, SLEEPING TOGETHER, skin to skin, losing it ... that's what's between these covers.

We expect our first slow dance or first kiss to be delicious, so why not expect the same from our first time having sex with someone?

If you're ready to have sex for the first time, or are wondering if you're ready, this book is written with you in mind. There are lots of fun, scary and weird things that you may want to know about. Maybe you're hoping for a "should-I-or-shouldn't-I?" quiz to help you figure out where you're at with the sex thing. It's all here! Or maybe it's not your first time, but it's your partner's first, and you want it to be amazing for them. Girls reading this may think, "doesn't happen like that with guys, not on this planet." Good news!! It can: I've had guys ask exactly that question about how to make it great on my Web site. Your interest in this topic may be piqued because you sense the time might be ripe for your friend or sib, and you'd like to help them figure out what's best for them and how to stay safe. And last but not least, you may have a parent or teacher who would like more info about this subject, so there's a chapter for them.

The Big Picture

For people under the age of twenty, especially if they own a vagina, lots of adults want to see "abstinence" as *the* talk. They believe that sex and youth only go together when the couple is married. Which should only happen when you're older. The thinking is that young people can't "handle" sex. This hasn't always been the case and isn't the case in certain cultures today. As Canadian researcher Eleanor Maticka-Tyndale points out, she knew of a case where it was very acceptable for a young woman to leave school and start a job at age fourteen, get married before she turned seventeen and have her first child before the age of eighteen. This was her grandmother, who was born in 1914! It was a common scenario back then.[1]

The point is that differences in thinking about when it's OK or not OK to start having sex are based not on facts about biology or readiness, but really on a specific group's social organization, how power and control over people are managed. Maticka-Tyndale refers to this as "political." In *The Women's History of the World,* author Rosalind Miles says that in every male-governed society, a husband "realized his divine right to a vacuum-sealed, factory fresh vagina ... purity guaranteed."[2]

> Adults often wonder what role the in-your-face hyper-sexual youth media plays in influencing young people's decisions. I've heard media described as a "mirror and a window": both reflecting a new reality and leading the way into it.

A totally different approach to "losing it" has been taken by villagers living in some South Pacific communities.[3] The Mangaians of the South Pacific encouraged young girls to explore their sexual pleasure on their own and with boys before they were allowed to get pregnant. Not that I'm suggesting that here (imagine the outcry); it's just to show that sex before marriage or at a certain age, by itself, is not going to destroy a person's life. You have to look at the whole picture.

And so you won't find me talking about abstinence. I don't even like the word. It's loaded with sex-negative tones. And what does it mean anyway? No wet kissing? Hands off each other's crotch? Is nipple nibbling OK? No oral sex allowed — or is it just no vaginal sex? What about a person who desires someone of the same sex?

Ready?

As you'll read in many parts of this book, I do have strong opinions about when people are or aren't ready to have sex. But my approach is, as we say in the sex (education) business, sex-friendly and gay-positive. From twenty years' experience in this field, I know that "Just Say No" doesn't help people wait until they're ready for sex. And that's what I'm after, helping you figure out if you're ready: the first time, but also each time after that. If your answer is "no, I'm not ready," then I have some suggestions on how to hang on awhile longer. If you answer "yes," then you can check out how to take the next steps safely. And if you're still confused ... read on!

Being "ready" isn't just a matter of age.

Technically, and according to the dictionary, losing your virginity is defined as "having had sexual intercourse." And sexual intercourse happens when "for purposes of procreation, a man's penis is inserted into a woman's vagina." Doesn't that sound appealing!? For some people, myself included, this definition is just a wee bit too narrow. Taken literally, it would mean that for people who were with someone of the same sex, no matter how sexually intimate they'd been, they'd still be virgins. How much sense does that make? I would at least expand the definition to include all genital penetration. Does that mean fingering "deflowers" a person? I don't think so, but I guess people can decide for themselves! I have to admit though: most questions that come my way about first-time sex have to do with vaginal intercourse between males and females. So, that's what I'll mainly be dealing with here.

If you're out of your teen years and still a "virgin" (maybe you're twenty-three and about to get married), nobody cares much if you have or haven't done it yet. In

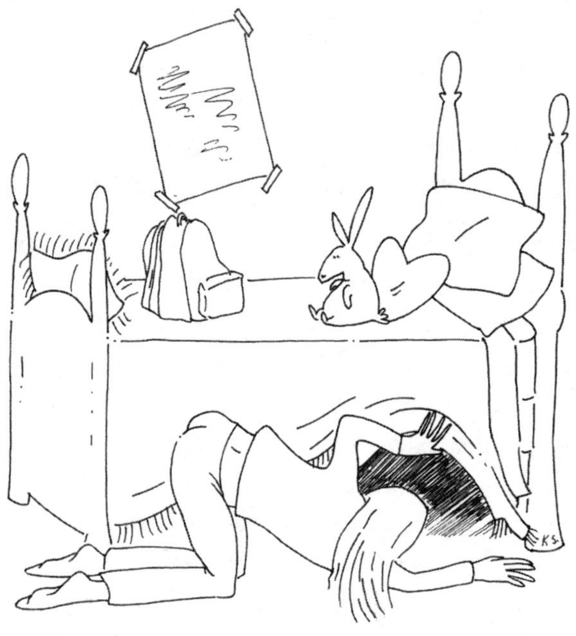

"Lost your virginity?"

fact, you'll find lots of people who won't believe that you haven't gone all the way! But you may still have lots of questions ...

Choice

The chapter called "Not Your Choice" is about being forced. I recognize that for many people, female and male, their "first time" experience was not their choice. They did not give consent. This needs to be a whole different kind of discussion. I have been part of those discussions and saw how talking about it helped the person who experienced the sexual coercion, abuse or assault.

> I was raped when I was thirteen. Now I have a boyfriend who really loves me. I like the affection [when having sex] and so I fake it [orgasm].
>
> — *JT (interviewed at age 16)*

Some people who are survivors of sexual abuse/assault define themselves as virgins until the time when *they* choose to have sex. If you or someone close to you has had to deal with this issue, it's crucial to get some help (if you haven't already) in order to enjoy your sexuality and have healthy relationships. For example, it would be very difficult for someone to enjoy their first time, consenting, if they'd not yet begun to deal with a previous experience of being forced or pressured. As with the young woman quoted above, there will still be sex — just not very good sex. To start the healing process, there are some suggested resources in the "Still Wondering ... More Info" chapter that may be helpful.

In *All The Way* I focus mainly on consenting sex. *Consent:* willing, wanting to do it, agreeing to do it. Fortunately, many people *do* have the choice of deciding when and where and with whom they'll share themselves. It's not always an easy thing to figure out, but it is a choice.

Not Just From My Head

Where did I get my material? Over the past years I've been sent lots of questions about this issue of first-time sex on my Web site sexscape.org. Stories and queries on this subject of going "all the way" have come to me through my work in clinics. The college course that I taught on human sexuality revealed lots of situations and concerns on this matter through my students' journals. This is one of the ways I happen to know that some college-age people (male and female) are still virgins (really, not everyone's done it by the end of high school!). I also had the pleasure of being part of a project where I was hired to do in-depth interviews with young women.

With all of this input, I still had the problem of hearing from way more young women than guys. To get around that, I took out an ad in a paper and got guys to tell me their stories. I spoke with lots of guys age eighteen to sixty. We had long and detailed conversations and lots of laughs. While guys (straight) are pretty shut-mouth about sharing the real goods on this subject, I found that once asked, even the guys in my everyday life were happy to tell all! Often "losing-your-virginity" stuff is just directed at females, but males (straight, gay or bi) have to deal with issues as well, even though these can differ from young women's.

ADULTS

The chapter "For Parents and Other Adults (Who Won't Be There)" exists because I do get questions from these (older) folks about how to help you make it through this stage in your life in one piece. Very often parents would like to see their kids wait for sex until they've finished their education, say ... age thirty! So they may be looking for tips on how to get you to wait till your older. As well, people who teach or work with youth get freaked by the number of teen pregnancies they see ... and then there's the skyrocketing infection rate!

Adults hear the regret from many young women (and some young men) who wish they'd waited till they were older before having sex, and have asked me how they can help someone make healthy choices when it comes to this decision. And these days there *are* adults who hope that the first time you have sex, it will be pleasurable as well as safe. At least a three or four star event!

Your questions about how to deal with parents and other adults can also be found in this chapter.

The Way It Is

There are people who say that if we returned to the "traditional" ways, things would be better. No more belly-button piercing or programs about birth control. What they're ignoring is that there have always been unwanted teen pregnancies, diseases and sexual abuse. In other times, people pretended this wasn't the case, and so the pregnancies were hidden or ended unsafely. At some points and places in history, sex outside marriage didn't happen as much, but when it was discovered, the shame and damage done (especially to the female) were brutal. Today, there are places in the world that are still like this, even while organizations fight to make it more just.

Since "popping the cork" happens to 94 percent of the population, why the fuss anyway? Again, for some people it's about following a strict set rules set out by their community. In some cultures, intercourse is seen as the cement that holds the two people together. No matter what your background, it is an event that you don't quickly forget. It's not like sharing an ice-cream cone. In fact, there wasn't anybody I spoke with who said, "hmmm, nope; I don't remember the first time." I guess the exceptions to this are if you were forced and too young or traumatized to remember, or you were so wasted it was all a blurrrr. The second reason you may want to pay attention when you take the plunge is that a bad time of it can set up some not-so-great patterns. For her, the classic is faking orgasms. For him, worries about "performance" or losing his erection can affect his sex life in the future.

By writing this book, am I encouraging you to, as they say, "screw your brains out"? To "go for it" before you're ready? No. I'm being realistic about the fact that lots of people start to have sex before their parents and health teachers would want them to. Definitely it often happens too soon. And there is no way of making it 100 percent safe. What part of living is? But as in any other situation, our choices are usually better if we're well informed and have had the chance to walk through what it would be like to say YES as well as NO. That's what this book is about.

KNOWLEDGE = POWER

So, I'd like to pass along some of the stories, wisdom, suggestions and funny things people have shared with me. One of my friends said, "Oh, isn't it kind of inevitable that sex for the first time is a let-down?" (She wasn't having a good day.) Forget that! I believe that with the right information, attitude and skills, first-time sex can be safe and fun.

You may notice that there are times in *All The Way* when I sound very easy-going, and other times I get kind of intense. That has to do with the roller-coaster nature of this subject. One minute you can be in the midst of a totally serious discussion about some aspect of sexuality, and the next moment you're killing yourself laughing. That's the way it is with this subject!

What *isn't* between these covers is a magic formula for you to figure out for sure what is *right for you* at this time. It's also not a sex guide that goes into detail about all the various kinds of sex, you know, feathers/S&M/threesomes ... sorry to disappoint! If you're interested in finding out more about other kinds of sex play, or anything else, you can check out the "Still Wondering ... More Info" chapter.

So, to sum it up, what you'll find in this book are ...

Facts about:

- ☆ BODIES, SEXUAL INTERCOURSE & (OF COURSE) PROTECTION FROM PREGNANCY AND STD/HIV

Stories from people who've:

- ☆ BEEN THERE AND WISHED THEY HADN'T
- ☆ BEEN THERE AND LIKED IT
- ☆ HAVE QUESTIONS ABOUT ALL SORTS OF SEX STUFF

Ideas on how to:

- ☆ COMMUNICATE ABOUT WHAT YOU WANT AS CLEARLY AS POSSIBLE.

My views on:

- ☆ HOW TO KNOW IF YOU'RE READY,
- ☆ SAFER SEX,
- ☆ WHAT TO EXPECT,

and

- ☆ GIVING YOURSELF MORE TIME.

CHAPTER 1

ready or not?

> How do you know when the right time to have sex is?
>
> — *grade six student*

> My girlfriend and I have been together for six months; we do everything but have sex. How can we know if we're ready?
>
> — *sexscape.org Web site, male, 15–20*

> I've been with this guy for awhile, and want to be ready, just in case, you know.
>
> — *clinic client, female, 17*

This question of "*when*" is the thing I get asked most consistently from people age ten to eighteen. The younger students aren't asking because of an immediate need to know (since sex = gross), but because it's in their face at every turn and they're curious. They are also, at their own rate, beginning to get those zinging feelings in their bodies. The older students are usually hot for somebody and trying to figure out how far to go. Often their body is saying, "YES, YES, YES" and their mind (for lots of girls and some guys too) is saying "I DUNNO." Many people told me that they sort of decided ahead of time when they'd start to have intercourse. For some it's when they get married. In Western culture, since the average age of marriage is in the late twenties, most don't wait that long. In spite of what we see around us, waiting *is* possible, as long as *both* people in the relationship have unwavering conviction. Waver and you're screwed, literally. Often this decision to wait is based on religious beliefs that the couple embraces, or strong societal controls.

bf/gf = boyfriend/girlfriend

Other people, again especially girls, have a predetermined plan. They decide that they'll wait till a certain age or stage in the relationship; until they've know their bf for six months, or the first time their parents go away overnight (!). For guys, the religious or education goals are sometimes present, but lots of guys have told me that the determining factor was how long before a willing partner turned up! Hmmmm.

Do these goal-setting plans work? Sometimes they do. Of course there are a ton of other things that get factored in during the real-life dance of when we end up "doing it" and with whom:

- The intoxicating feeling (sorry, but that's all it is ...) of falling in love for the first time.
- Feeling the need to touch and be touched, other than patting your family pet.
- Pressure because of what your friends are doing, and you're not.
- The intoxicating feeling of being intoxicated (drunk) or high.
- Deciding to exchange sex for something you want.
- To prove that you're no longer a kid.
- To prove you're straight.
- Wanting to please.
- Being defiant.
- New Year's.
- Curiosity.
- Grad.

(Or just because you are *soooo* horny you can't even put your shoes on without connecting it to doin' the wild thing).

Some people tell me that you should just let sex happen: "Don't think about it so much." Well, besides the fact that it's my job to think about it (!), there are some obvious problems with just letting nature have its way. People's lives can be wrecked. Everybody is aware of the threat of an accidental pregnancy or sexually transmitted infection (STI). We just never think it will happen to us. But it does — all the time. That's why there are separate chapters on these things!

The other damage that can happen is emotional. If you don't give anything of your "self" emotionally when you have sex, then you're not going to lose much (or gain much). But if you allow yourself to really connect with someone, if you feel strongly for him or her, then you may learn what a heart-break feels like. If you break up, if they are very critical towards you, if they cheat on you — it will hurt like hell! Thinking and talking about stuff ahead of time can't always prevent the damage — but it can reduce the risks.

I know, enough talk — how do you know the RIGHT TIME? Let's make it simpler by using the "who, when, where" approach. The "how" is a whole separate chapter!

WHO?

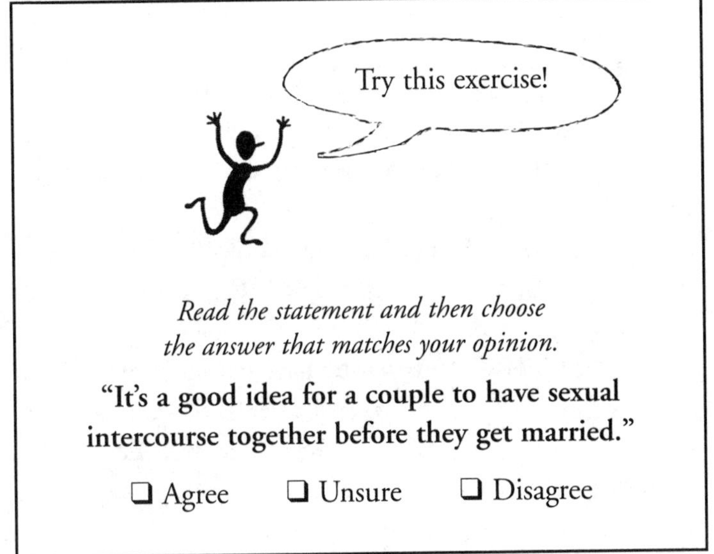

Read the statement and then choose the answer that matches your opinion.

"It's a good idea for a couple to have sexual intercourse together before they get married."

❑ Agree ❑ Unsure ❑ Disagree

Which opinion would you tick off? Why? The college students that I do this exercise with, who are from all different backgrounds, mostly choose the "**Agree**" category. As one really sensitive guy explained, "it's like buying a car: you want to test drive it first."

For those who choose the "**Unsure**" category, a young woman said, "It worked out fine for me and my boyfriend, but I can't say for other people." Someone else added, "It depends on what other experiences you've had; in some cases I think you can know just by kissing the guy."

And from the few people in the "**Disagree**" group, the opinion was, "I believe that it's best for a couple to wait until marriage; this is a precious thing that they should discover together."

We know that just because someone has had lots of lovers, that doesn't make them good at it! Just like some people will stay so-so basketball players all their lives no matter how many teams they play with... It's true that there are some compatibility issues such as genital size (though most of us are one-size-fits-all) and level of horniness. However, many things change with time, and a good long-term sex life together mostly has to do with talking openly, sticking with your commitment and being willing to risk by trying something new now and then!

So, some of you will wait until you're wed. This is often the case when people embrace their religious teachings on celibacy, have education as a priority or want to show this kind of respect to their future wife/husband. For sure sexism often enters the picture. In many cultures it's really only the woman who is supposed to remain "pure." There is often not the same pressure or expectation for guys.

> I was twenty-one, from a Catholic family, and wanted to wait until marriage, so we had done everything-but. Our honeymoon was very intimate and special. It was somewhat uncomfortable [physically]. My husband wasn't a virgin.
>
> — *"Angie," interview*

If you're like the majority of people reading this book, having sex for the first time is not going to happen on your wedding night. According to stats, you'll likely end up making love to a bf/gf who you've known for awhile, rather than someone unknown.

> It was nice; it was his first time too, and I loved him ... we were totally relaxed.
>
> — *IT, female (was 17)*

There are definitely advantages to being with someone you know versus someone you hardly know at all. Go ahead and make your own list ...

____

____

____

____

____

____

____

Here's mine:

1. For women it's true that it's guys we know who do most of the sexual assault/rapes. But at least you have some chance at sniffing out the creeps if you've spent some time with them first.
2. You have some idea of how trustworthy (old-fashioned, eh?) the other person is or isn't. For instance, do they call when they say they will? Do they keep personal info about you and others private?
3. Lots of people look forward to emotional closeness, not just "banging." Tough to get this with someone you've just met.
4. You know who to call if you don't use a condom and end up getting a gross looking/smelling vaginal discharge and a slight fever in the next two weeks!! (The gift that keeps on giving ...)

Just knowing someone doesn't mean that they're the person your parent(s) or best friend would want you to be with! It doesn't always end up like a fairy tale. Say they're really selfish, or unreliable. But you still want to be with them, 'cause you're a crazy human, just like the rest of us! In this case, be as realistic as you can. DON'T EXPECT TOO MUCH. It's not like what happens in movies; they're not going to suddenly transform just because you care about them. They're just as likely not to show up for your "special" time together, or if they do, they'll flick on the game minutes afterwards, or get on the phone with a friend.

Sometimes people end up having sex for the first time with a friend. They may be the same or the opposite sex. Sexual play may be an extension of their friendship. The intimacy, attraction and playfulness that created the relationship act as a natural shift to more "hands-on" exploration! As AJ, who was seventeen when she did it with a guy friend said, "It felt comfortable. I trusted him ... We became fuck-buddies." On the other hand, AS told me that she felt that it "didn't count, 'cause it was just curiosity, no other feelings involved." When the sex continues, people are usually friends first, lovers second. While this can be a safe way to lose it, it *can* be tricky, particularly when one person gets more emotionally involved or has a bf/gf.

You may choose to have sex with someone you've just met. There's a total thrill being with someone new. Their smell, voice and touch. For a female, being with an unknown person is still considered a no-no by society, kind of slutty, 'cause you don't have any relationship other than — sex! Blows away the love + sex equation. For some, the risk-taking and taboo add an extra kick to the experience. Sort of like extreme sports.

> It was great, a New Year's party; we'd just met that evening!
>
> — *WR, male (was 18)*

Some people really don't care very much about who they end up with, because they just want to "get it done." While it's not what I'd hope for for someone, I guess the

advantage is that there's not the whole thing of figuring out a new way of being together afterwards. And if the experience is not a pleasure, you don't have to deal with it. If it's fireworks — bonus. Maybe you'll end up seeing each other again. But that's not usually the goal ...

And not everybody hopes that the first time will be enjoyable. Some women expect it to be painful and/or a let-down. This often leads to the just-get-it-over-with approach.

There are times when someone may have to, or may decide to, have sex in order to get some material thing. It could be a place to sleep, some food, drugs, tickets to a concert, or a shopping spree. As long as people feel that they have a choice, I think it's up to them how and why they decide to "lose it." Unfortunately, even when it *is* their choice, the deal often does not include safer sex.

If you end up being with someone you don't really know, one young woman said that it's best to have a friend not too far away, like under the bed! Speak up for yourself right off, listen to your gut and use your voooice.

For social and safety reasons, choosing to be with someone unknown may not be quite the same for girls as it is for guys.

For more on being pressured into having sex, and on safety suggestions, see the chapter "Not Your Choice."

Age

WHATAGEWHATAGEWHATAGEWHATAGEWHATAGE?

What's the legal age of consent to have intercourse? Depends on what country or state you're living in. And regardless of the age of consent, in most places, people like a coach or teacher who are in charge of young people can't have sex with them.

Country/State	Age of Consent for Sex
Canada	12–14 years with conditions,* otherwise 14. Anal: age 18.
United States	16–19 years depending on the state. Anal: usually 18 or totally illegal.
Denmark	15 years old for everything.
England	16 years old for everything.

* As long as the older person isn't more than two years older, so 14 and 16 is OK; 14 and 17 is not.

"Girls — they're looking for Mr. Right; but guys are looking for Miss Right Now."[4]

> Once guys find out [you're a virgin], they want to break it — so I just kept away.
>
> — *JR (was 19 and still a virgin)*

Are all guys "horny dogs" only interested in one thing!? No. But when you're young, you don't have enough experience to handle those guys who *do* operate this way!

So, if you just want to "lose it," then the age of the other person won't really matter. But if you want some *sweet lovin'*, it takes confidence and openness. Being a bit older your first time doesn't guarantee anything, but it often helps.

When's the normal time to start having sex?
— *grade ten girls' class*

In Canada, about half of teens have had vaginal intercourse by age seventeen. In the USA, it depends more on which group of youth you're talking about, but it's about the same, with about 70 percent active in grade twelve.[5] But that stat is not going to help *you* figure out how old *you* should be, right? Instead, let me tell you what people have been telling me from their own experience.

We did a school survey with fourteen- to fifteen-year-olds and asked, "If you haven't had sexual intercourse yet, what are your reasons?" Many of the guys' answers went something like, "Because I haven't had a chance yet." (Thanks, guys.) Other reasons they gave? Some want to wait until they're married. Yes, it's true. More want to wait until they're with someone they care about — so it's not just about getting laid. Others say they want a certain amount of their education finished, in case ... well, you know the rest.

As I mentioned before, some people are really specific with their start time ...

Not till age eighteen.

After I've started college/university.

When we've been together at least six months.

On my honeymoon.

My best friend and I have agreed that we'll both wait until the end of grade ten.

Do people stick to these goals? No surprises here — yes and no. **Generally, the women and girls I've spoken with who started sleeping with guys at an early age wished that they'd waited.** "So, what's early?" you ask. They were often age thirteen to fifteen ... And I agree that's too early for intercourse. Not too early for some making out and learning about pleasure, but for going all the way.

> I was scared I'd lose my boyfriend [age seventeen] ... Later, that's all we ever did and I usually faked it ... It made breaking up harder.
>
> — *DD, on having sex at 14*

Who needs that!! I guess there are some younger girls who are really pleased with the who, when, where, why and all that, but in twenty years of talking about this, I've not run into many! Being older doesn't mean it's going to be great, but for girls, it's likely to be better.

Many, *many* young women say that they wished they'd waited until they were a bit older, "ready for it." Girls often end up with a guy who is a bit older than them. He may have already done it, or at least she thinks he probably has and so she feels pressure. As I've said, there is lots of pressure to have sex before you're really ready, no matter whether you're a guy or a girl.

And What Would A Doctor Say?

For young women, the cells on the cervix do not finish maturing until the *late teens*. There is a relationship between early intercourse and a higher chance of getting cervical cancer later in life.

— teen clinic doctor

Many health experts now believe that cervical cancer is mainly caused by exposure to a sexually transmitted infection (STI) called the human papilloma virus (HPV). Since condoms are seldom consistently used by younger teen girls, they are at high risk for getting HPV. The combination of having cervical cells that are still maturing/changing with having HPV is not good. We are seeing more and more young women whose cervical cell tests (Pap tests) come back "abnormal." This doesn't mean that all of these young women will go on to develop cancer, but they are at increased risk.

Not all types of HPV are linked with cancer of the cervix.

Is it true that women's sexual peak is in their thirties, guys in their teens?

— *teen group*

This idea of "sexual peak" gets tossed around a lot. I get a bit worried that someone may end up thinking that they've either "missed the boat" or are waiting for their "ship to come in!" Don't pay too much attention to this age thing. There are lots of kinds of "peaks" — when you're most fertile, when you feel the horniest, when it's easiest to orgasm, and when you enjoy sex the most. For any one person these all may happen at different ages! This means that instead of there being any "best" age to be having sex, it comes back to what's best for *you*, in *your* life.

Generally, unless you want a dozen kids, there are more advantages to waiting till you're at least in your later teens. At that time, we're more comfortable with our bodies and, especially for females, better at knowing what turns us on and how to get that happening! And that's when guys are more likely to pay attention to pleasing. Now *that's* the "peak" you want to hit!

"SO OK, HOW DO I KNOW THE RIGHT TIME!!!!?"

- You're at least age sixteen (in my opinion ...) and females know the cervical cancer stuff.
- You've done lots of making out, talked about protection (from babies and/or infections), and have protection ready. For guys, you've practised with a condom before — alone.

- You don't have to keep asking yourself and others this question!
- You can sit at the side of the tub shaving your legs and chatting with the guy (or girl).
- You can imagine doing it sober with the lights on and your clothes off.
- YOU FEEL LIKE IT *REALLY* IS YOUR CHOICE — TO DO IT OR NOT DO IT.
- You ______________________ (how would *you* know?)

> Wait six months from the time you think you want to do it, and then see how you feel. If it still seems like a good idea, fine.
>
> — *SF, a single mom who had her child at 21*

I think this is wise advice. It saves lots of regret if people, especially young women and those not sure about their sexual orientation, wait for a while before jumping into this messy part of life. Even without any scary stuff in the picture (such as feeling pressured or all the STIs), you'll have a better chance of having a good time!

Age Differences

Does the age of the person you're with make a difference? It can. If one person is more than a couple of years older than

Studies have also shown that if a guy is more than four years older than his girlfriend, and she gets pregnant, she's more likely to end up as a mother (a single mother), than if the couple are closer in age. Couples who are closer in age are also more likely to use condoms.

the other, the one who is younger (usually the girl) often feels pressure. The pressure doesn't just come from him; she also puts pressure on herself 'cause she doesn't want to feel different from her friends or from what she thinks is "normal."

I kept comparing myself to his last girlfriend.

— DD, 17 (first time at age 14)

I've heard an interesting thing from guys about the age of their first lover. Guys with a girlfriend around their own age described the experience as "quick" and that it "felt right." But I also ended up interviewing lots of guys who had been with a female at least two years older than they were. What they said was that the age factor seemed important in helping to make their first time awesome. Jake, who was fifteen, was with a woman five years older, and he said that it was "heavenly." James, age fourteen, who was with a friend (female) age seventeen, said that the experience was "thrilling; so exciting I couldn't think." Now, this was not a proper survey and I know it's not always the case, but I have to say that girls who ended up with older guys did not use the same kinds of descriptions!

There are some obvious reasons as to why men and women often describe first-time intercourse quite differently. First, guys don't have to worry about the pain factor, so they can focus on the pleasure part more. They're also not usually so mindful of pregnancy or "what my parents would think." If a young man is with someone older (i.e. more experienced), it takes the pressure off about knowing what to do. She's more likely to be on top of the protection issue. And finally, a lover who is somewhat older will likely be more confident and able to say/show what she likes. Nothing sexier than that!

Am I suggesting that guys seek out an older partner? Wouldn't that get me into trouble! Maybe if *this* was the norm, rather than the guy being the older partner, then guys would be taught to be great lovers and their future partner(s) would benefit!! This notion was likely behind the custom that led fathers in some cultures to take their sons to a prostitute for their "initiation." Not so great in my opinion. Actually, my point is (you've been patient) that the male or the female partner being older *can* make a difference, in various ways. How do *you* think it would affect *you?*

When?

Timing. People (of all ages) wonder how long you should be going out with someone before you decide to have sex. This is assuming it is a *decision*, and not something that "just happens." Nobody can say you have to wait so many months or years — because it will depend on you and who you're with. Realistically, in order to have enough trust and communication happening, I'd think at least six months needs to be spent together. Seems that the younger you are, the more time this would take to establish.

A survey of 512 youth in the USA, ages fifteen to seventeen, shows respondents thought most couples who have intercourse should wait two to twelve months before doing it.[6]

Once you've decided you're ready to do "the wild thing," you may want to let it happen "whenever," you may plan it all out, or you may do a bit of both. Of course, on lots of TV shows and movies, people don't seem to plan sex; it "just happens" in an explosion of passion. And mostly at night, right? In real life, especially for young people, that's not often the case. Too many people around at night! This accounts for the very popular after-school-before-mom-gets-home liaison. At least parents can't get after you for sitting around and watching TV until supper! I don't advise sneaking sex in while you're supposed to be, for instance, babysitting.

And late at night when one or both of you has been partying is, as one guy put it, "a waste." This last category probably *includes* wedding nights, if you go the big party route. Instead, choose a time when you're not stressed or rushed. Later, a quickie in the shower or back seat is totally fun ... but not for your first time.

I'm constantly hearing about people who plan their first time around a special event — New Year's, a birthday, Grad night. What do you think about this idea? At least they're doing some planning. But it can be a set-up for major disappointment, given all the people who may be around, and the partying. For girls, I wonder if it just gives them the excuse they're looking for. Or is it more caving in to pressure? See below and page 165 for more on this.

WHERE?

In the movie *Titanic,* they did it in a car. Well, in a car on a boat. There are jokes about "in the bush" or "a roll in the hay" and that was where quite a few of the people that I've spoke with had their first time. There was also the cottage, the beach, hotels, campus residence, in tents ...

Of course there are hotel rooms. People think of this option as fun, cheesy, embarrassing, expensive or all of the above! At least it offers some privacy. For those still in high school, rooms are often booked for after the school grad or formal. If you're thinking of "going for it" as part of a prom/graduation celebration, here's some advice from those who've been there …

> It's nice if it's with your boyfriend, someone special. As long as you don't get wasted, 'cause then it's, like, no point …
>
> — *SG, 18*

> If you don't want to do it that night, then don't get a room alone; also you need to be honest with your date.
>
> — *FF, 17*

What about weekend parties?

> It happened at a friend's party; I was around sixteen. We were both drinking and I just wanted to do it, to, like, get it over with. It wasn't great, for sure.
>
> — *SP, 21*

Yuck. Even if you don't really care about being with someone "special," you can do way better than tanked at a party! If you're a guy, you may think, "that's the only time girls are OK with going all the way." I'd love to say "wrong," but in lots of cases you'd be right! Things that people have mixed feelings about — like going to a party, getting up and dancing, or having sex — get smoothed over when enough alcohol is added. Lots of women (younger and older) allow themselves to be "swept away." And sometimes guys take advantage of the altered state that females find themselves in. If you're wasted, then things "just happen." Fact is, if you're drunk or high, you can't legally give/get consent to sexual intercourse.

Statistically though, "first times" happen mostly at home, his or hers. As one young woman reminded me, this includes the garage (in the car)! I'd avoid apartment building garages ... At home you have at least some chance for privacy. Condoms can easily be stashed somewhere, though what to do with the used ones and wrappers has to be considered. Don't flush them; the plumber's bill won't be the only cost! The question about getting your parents' consent to have your bf/gf stay over can be checked out in the "For Parents and Others" chapter.

Looking at the *who, when* and *where* questions may have helped you see where you're going, or wanting to go, with this part of your life. If you think that you'll likely end up having sex sooner rather than later, then I invite you to carry on through the following chapters. If you're thinking, "no way, not yet!", the next section is for you!

Not (Yet ...)

> My most embarrassing time came when I was making out watching TV with this totally hot guy. He was the best kisser. It just felt like we were melting into each other. Nobody was around. I had never had sex and I didn't plan to do it with him, but I didn't want to stop either. He started to undo his pants and I jumped up, saying someone might come home. I felt freaked out. He zipped up, then was lying on top of me while we touched, and he suddenly stopped. He sat up and I could see this big dark wet spot on his jeans. We were both so embarrassed. I couldn't say anything, so we just sat and watched some dumb program.
>
> — CM

While CM's situation was embarrassing, at least it didn't end in a real disaster. She might have let herself be "swept away" and had sex without any protection. The guy might have gotten really pushy and not listened to her "not-here-not-now." They might have been "caught"! The same scene could have happened between two guys or two girls as well.

So how could CM's sweet evening have ended differently? What could they do next time? Would any of these ideas work? ⇩

a. Avoid spending lots of time *alone* at home (car, park ...) making out — boring but very effective.
b. Talk about how far you're OK going *before* you get there. CM could have said, "Slow down, big guy; I'm not even close to going there."
c. If you're too shy to "use your words," then use body language (like keeping both people's hands above the hips, pants done up ...).
d. Watch something more interesting on TV.

Again, because someone wants to wait to have intercourse doesn't necessarily mean no touching. People have found other ways to share physical pleasure, including things like "breast sex" and love bites.

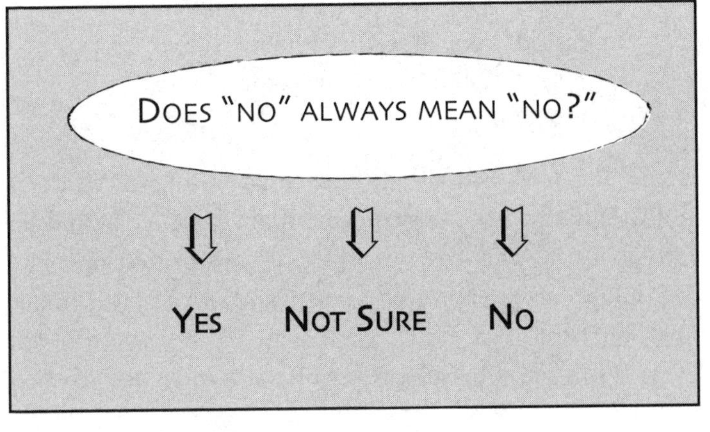

Guys tell me that a "no" often means "not yet," "not here," or "convince me." If you're a female reading this, you may feel pissed off — because for you it's important for "no" to mean "no." There are some jerks out there who don't take "no" for an answer, but that's not usually the case. Often guys are confused. And who can blame them! Sometimes when a girl says "no," she means these other things. Why the mixed message? Because we live in a world of "double standards." There's one set of rules for guys and another for girls. So, it's how the game often goes: advance-retreat-advance-give in. The girl may worry that if she seems too eager, the guy will think she's a ho or experienced. She/he may be nervous. She may not have totally decided what she wants and so gives mixed messages. What's the solution to this mess?

- Make your "yes" a "yes" and your "no" a "no." (Ignore the "ho-ho-ho" or "cock-tease" labels that might happen.) *If you feel unsure about having sex, then it's totally fine to stop at any point.*
- If you're getting mixed signals from your partner, slow down! Sure, they may be into what's going on, but that doesn't mean they're OK with going further. Better to say, "OK, I'm confused about what you want; should we stop?" Trying to read someone's mind is not the same as getting *consent.*

The fact is, we're all programmed to have sex, so if you're going to wait, it takes some planning. If you figure you're going to get "friendly" with someone, but don't want to go all the way, here are some questions you can think about:

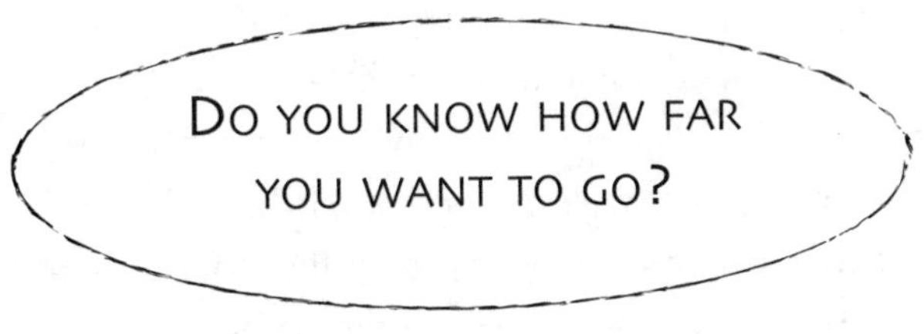

DO YOU KNOW HOW FAR
YOU WANT TO GO?

If you can answer "yes" to this, then I strongly suggest you let the person you're hot for know the answer — *before* you have any clothes off! I know they never talk about this stuff in movies or on TV, but real life is different. Talking can be a bit awkward, but not as awkward as what can happen if nothing is said, like what happened in CM's story (above). If the answer is, "I don't know," that's fair, because with new experiences, we often don't know how we feel until we're actually there. The only problem is if you just take things as they come (so to speak) — our feelings can become really powerful and drown out our thinking. This is especially true if you're drunk or high. I've had a ton of young people into clinic for pregnancy and STD tests who have said that sex "just happened." And I know that it *can* happen like that — but it doesn't have to.

How and when do you let the other person know how far you're going to go?

When to talk ... during a phone call? Flirting online? On your way to their house, the park, or wherever? Once you're messing around and feeling totally horny? *You* need to decide, especially if you don't know the other person really well. Often, because this isn't the most comfortable thing to talk about, it's easier to joke, or use terms that the two of you have worked out. One young woman said, "Wait till the time feels right to talk." My worry with that advice is that for some people, there never seems to be a "natural" time, so the talking never happens. The same person suggested choosing a time when you're feeling close, when you're just cuddling. Since we don't usually hear about how other people work this stuff out, you may think that anything you say will sound like a movie from health class — but you have to say *something!* Otherwise it all becomes a guessing game, and you can lose big-time.

Let's talk about
sex, baby.

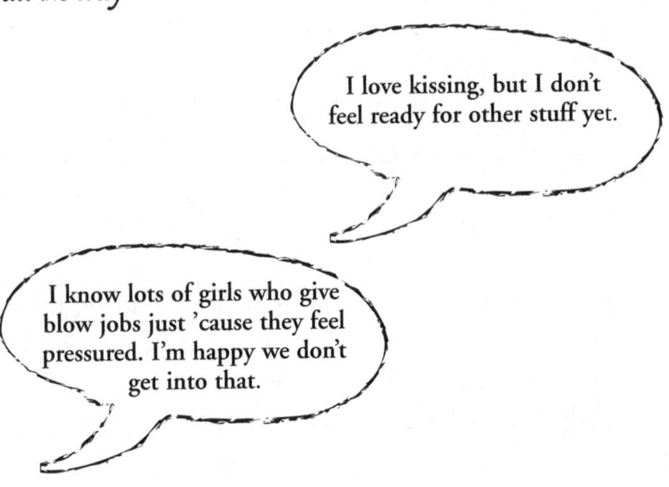

I love kissing, but I don't feel ready for other stuff yet.
I know lots of girls who give blow jobs just 'cause they feel pressured. I'm happy we don't get into that.

If you put some limits on how far you want to go and the other person responds with something like "take it easy ... nothing will happen," and you feel like they're kind of putting you down, alarm bells should be going off in your head: stay clear.

If you're a guy putting the brakes on, there's a whole different game. Because you're "supposed" to charge ahead,

if you don't, some girls (or guys) may end up using loaded lines like, "I thought you were into me" (guilt) or "What's wrong?" (you have a problem). They may hint that you're gay (or straight, if you're with another guy). Again, the only way you can hope to make it OK is to figure out what you want and then talk about it.

You don't *have* to say why you've set certain limits. You may not even have a "reason," just a feeling, and that's fine!

For something as natural as sex, I'm sure I make this sound complicated! If, at home or in school, you get the chance to talk about the kinds of real-life situations involving relationships and sexual things, it can make this time of life easier. Unfortunately, that's not often the case. So you talk with your friends, or keep the struggles to yourself. Sharing our thoughts and feelings with the person we're hot for is not always the easiest thing. The good news is that it gets easier with more practice! If you're not able to talk, waiting to have sex until *you* are ready can be tricky. Don't stay silent and let it just happen — that's crappy. It's OK to get your own way with this!

CHAPTER 2

not your choice

Consent: (to) express willingness, give permission, agree.

Coerce: persuade or restrain (an unwilling person) by force.

Think about the last time you went out with your friends. Whatever you ended up doing — seeing a movie, just hanging out at someone's place — was it something you agreed to do or did you get dragged along or talked into it? For all of us, there are definitely times when we get pressured into doing something we don't really want to do. That's called coercion. We may "go along" with it, but it's because we're feeling pressured. Some of you reading this book may have been, or still are, in a situation where sexual activity is coercive — in some way forced. This means there was not (or is not) freely given agreement. This kind of sexual violation can happen to people of any age, either gender.

Whether you're a kid or grown up, it hardly needs to be said that there can be negative effects from forced sexual contact. People find that by talking about the abuse, the effects can be lessened. And while there is no way of absolutely preventing sexual abuse/assault from happening, the chances can be reduced through knowledge and awareness.

As a Child

When he was a child, "MJ" lived with his parents and two brothers. They were just a regular family. He did OK in school and had a couple of good friends. All his life a family friend, "Uncle" Joe, visited regularly. He brought the boys treats; they liked him. Starting when MJ was around age five, Uncle Joe would go into MJ's room to say goodnight. When MJ was in bed, Uncle Joe would give him a back rub, including his bottom. He then started a game where, for a "prize," he'd have MJ touch his penis. In time this progressed to oral sex. Uncle Joe said that this was a game that lots of guys played. As MJ got older, Uncle Joe would show him porn videos when they were alone. Through all of this, Uncle Joe used bribes and guilt to convince MJ to keep their "games" a secret. When he was able to, MJ moved away from home and from the city where his "uncle" lived. Later, because of his heavy drinking and problems with his girlfriend, MJ went to a counselling centre and talked about his story.

Fortunately, most of us do not have to deal with this kind of unwanted sexual attention.

Unfortunately, it is more common than we think, and it mainly happens with someone the person who is abused knows. The abuser may not necessarily be someone who's older or bigger than the person who is abused. For example, one kid may trick, bribe and/or pressure another kid into doing sexual things they don't really want to do.

> "**Survivor**" is a term used to describe a person who was a victim of sexual abuse/assault. People may wait many years before they decide they need to go and talk with someone about the abuse that happened to them as a child.

Having something sexual done *to* you can affect a person in lots of different ways[7]:

- There may not be any serious effect on a child, especially if the assault/abuse didn't go on for a long time. There may be less of an effect as well if there was no penetration or if the child told someone and the person she/he talked to believed him or her. Sometimes, though, what seems like nothing to the person hearing the story seems *huge* to the kid.

- A person who was sexually abused may find it hard to touch or be touched in an affectionate way. As an adolescent or adult, he or she may have sexual problems.
- Teens or adults who were sexually abused may find they feel like they have no control over their sexual behaviour. They may end up having sex with lots of people and may not use protection.
- When they grow up, they may have trouble with depression. They may have low self-esteem, an eating disorder, or serious problems with alcohol and other drugs.
- Some women who were sexually abused as children get abused in all sorts of different ways as they grow up, including sexually. This may be the case with guys as well.

Just because some people are really affected by sexual abuse in these ways doesn't mean that *everyone* is. You can do OK in the end. Again, by confronting the past and getting help with it, lots of people have said that surviving the violation made them into stronger people.[8] There are many different ways that people find to heal.

If you are ready to get help, **you can talk to someone you trust or call a distress line, a sexual abuse hot-line or kids' help line.**

When people's first sexual experiences are forced, they often don't count it as their *real* first time. Since good sex is something that two people do *together*, focusing on the consensual first time makes a lot of sense.

-I Guess one day-

I guess one day maybe
I will get over this
I hope each day and until then my pain is real
I Can't erase the past
I'm working on the future
I Know what happened to me
You will not make me weak
I'm beautiful and smart
You once made me ugly
I hate how you treated me and now you will pay
I don't know what I'll do but
I hope your conscience might help
Tell me how does it feel to just take and not care?
Tell me how do you walk and keep your head high
Are you proud of yourself?

-Anonymous 16-

As a Teen or Adult

People often call it rape. That's the term people generally use when someone is forced to have intercourse. However, just like the previous story about MJ, there are lots of other kinds of sexual activities that disregard a person's wishes but don't involve intercourse. In many countries, the broader term "sexual assault" is used for unwanted intercourse as well as any other kind of unwanted sexual activity.

> **Sexual assault:** Any nonconsensual sexual activity ranging from unwanted touching, to forced oral, anal or vaginal intercourse, to sexual violence in which the victim is wounded or maimed or his/her life is endangered.[9]

His Story/Her Story

I'd known Tanya for a while because we had some of the same friends. One weekend, I went away with a bunch of friends to this cottage, and she was there. We spent the day checking each other out, flirting and stuff. That night there was an amazing party — we were both drinking and ended up dancing together. Later, when she said she was going back to her cabin, I walked her. She seemed ready for anything. I went in with her and we started to make out. She was so hot. When I undid my pants, she laughed and said I'd better not, that she wasn't "on" anything. I told her not to worry. She made some other excuses and I figured she was just wanting me to take the lead, so I did. It seemed like she had as much fun as me, but the next day she left without saying anything. What the hell?

When I saw that JB was up at the cottage the weekend I was there, my heart skipped a beat. All of us thought he was so hot. The day was great — swimming and flirting my butt off. That night at the party we both had a lot to drink and danced, mostly together. I was wiped out, so I headed back to the cabin before my friends. JB came with me, and we ended up making out, which was fine — at first. I heard him unzip his pants and got nervous. I didn't want to have sex; I also didn't want to totally turn him off. My head was spinning from the beer. I couldn't make him understand that I didn't want to go further. He was really intense and I got frightened, so I just let him do it. The next day I felt so disgusted and angry — I left as soon as I could.

Date rape usually happens guy-on-girl. It could happen girl-on-guy (especially when a girl shames him into it), girl-on-girl or guy-on-guy. When it's guy-on-girl, most of the time it involves a guy the girl knows or is already with.

Often these guys just don't see it as assault. Just like in JB's story, the guy would say to himself that maybe the girl put up a bit of resistance so that she wouldn't look too experienced, but that he *knew* she "wanted it."

Meantime, the young woman is left feeling totally degraded, confused and embarrassed. She often feels as if it was her fault because of where she was, how she was dressed, or what she had already let him do. However, forced sexual activity is *never her fault.* Maybe, looking back, she could have protected herself better or had her radar turned on to "high," but she was not responsible for the assault. To have consensual (agreed to) sex, both people must "express willingness" as the definition says. If one person hesitates, says, "I'm not sure," pulls away, or anything like that — that's a "NO." This applies even if she/he's stripped naked and has a condom ready to go. It doesn't matter. If there's any confusion — and there sure can be with people who at first say "yes, yes, yes" and then "no, no, no" — *stop the action.* A guy needs to *ask*, "Do you want to do this?" It may sound like a dumb idea, but it's the only way he can be sure!

> When I was around seventeen, I'd often end up having sex with guys when I really didn't want to. I'd say "no" and then they'd keep talking and doing stuff, and I'd go along with it. I'd just lie there until they were done; I'd leave and regret what happened. But then it would happen again. I don't know why I did it. It wasn't assault, because I let it happen. I didn't get up and leave.
>
> — *TS, male, 30*

While "TS" feels that he was to blame for what happened, because he could have left, he was in fact verbally manipulated into it — "persuaded by force." Sex happened *to* him. That's why he felt crappy afterwards. Maybe he didn't say "no," but he sure didn't say "yes" either. You can never feel good about any sexual touching when you don't really want it.

CAUTION:

It may be risky to be with someone you hardly know if you're young, like under sixteen. I know this may sound totally obvious ... but usually you're more or less alone with a guy when you're making out. And so you are more at risk for sexual assault. Certain guys will take advantage of your gender (if female), your inexperience and your age. Even if you want to go all the way, they're more likely to push you into having sex without a condom, or to do stuff you're probably not ready for, like full-on anal sex.

If you are sexually assaulted and especially if there was forced oral, vaginal or anal sex, you need help — both medical attention and someone to listen to you, so you can start to believe it wasn't your fault. You may need emergency contraceptive pills (also called the "Morning-After" pill) to prevent pregnancy. You may need antibiotics in case he had an STD like chlamydia. (See the "Infections" chapter.) You may want to have an HIV test and then another one in three months. If it's positive in three months, you'll know it was from him.

Here is something you need to know. If you are under sixteen, and you get help at a sexual health clinic, a hospital or a sexual assault care centre, they have to call a child protection agency like the Children's Aid Society. If you are over sixteen and you want to report this crime to the police, the grrrls who wrote the *Little Black Book*[10] have a list of suggestions to consider:

- Go to a sexual assault clinic where there will be properly trained counsellors and medical staff ready to help you. Depending on the situation, you may need emergency contraceptive pills (ECP or "Morning-After" pills) and/or STI (infection) treatment.
- Try to get someone you trust and feel comfortable with to go with you.
- If you think you might go to a clinic, don't bathe or shower. It may be hard to not clean yourself because you may feel dirty, but it is important that you don't. There may be evidence on your body from the person who assaulted you that can be collected and used against him in court.
- Keep track of everything that happened, and who you talk with, *in writing*.

Sometimes people who've been assaulted don't want to go to the police. They may be embarrassed, afraid, or think they won't be believed. Even if you don't want to go to the police, someone else can do a "third-party report" for you. They don't give your name, but the police get the information. Then they can check to see if there is a crime pattern. Maybe this guy has done it before.

If date rape ever happens to you, you have some choices about what to do and whom to tell. It's very common to stay quiet and not tell anyone. But you know what?

Talking about it to a professional can really help. There are numbers in the "Still Wondering ... " chapter.

Some ideas the *Little Black Book* grrrls had for trying to avoid assault include:

- **Buddy system** — agree to watch out for each other when you're partying.
- Be aware of **Rohypnol** — this is one of several date rape drugs can be slipped into a drink. Keep an eye on your drink: toss it if it tastes odd or salty.
- **Sexist comments** — they can be a signal that a guy doesn't respect females: stay clear.
- **Wendo** — this is a self-defense course for women. It starts by encouraging women to be very aware of their environment — to avoid isolated places etc.
- **Fight back! Shout!** 70 percent of women who fight back scare the guy and don't get raped.

If you're the one who has manipulated or pressured somebody into doing something sexual, you also have a bunch of choices. You can continue to think you did nothing wrong. Or, if you admit that you used force, you can blame the person you assaulted: "she was a cock-tease." Or you can admit that your actions were wrong. This is the first huge positive step. Admitting this to the person you assaulted is the next challenge. If police were involved, you need to contact them. And finally, you need to go and talk to a professional so that you don't repeat the pattern in the future, which is very likely if you don't change the way you think about what happened.

One of the toughest questions I get asked is, *Why would someone do that to another person?* There isn't just one straightforward reason. Research has found that men who sexually "take" from others without their consent have come from a background of neglect and/or abuse.[11] Often this was physical or emotional abuse when they were kids. Having control or power over someone else becomes *really important to them — like an obsession* as they grow up. Also, in our society, males in general are encouraged to be aggressive and to "take control." For some guys, this means being aggressive sexually.

The research also says that when you sexually control someone, versus physically assaulting them, *you are more likely to get away with it* with no consequence to you. Two more things that increase the likelihood of a guy's being coercive are if he "has trouble expressing his feelings ... [and] is insensitive to others' feelings."

For people (males and females) who sexually abuse kids, there is also often a strong sexual turn-on they have towards children, screwed up as that sounds. As well, they have lost that inner voice that usually makes us act in a socially acceptable way. They are out of control and need help.

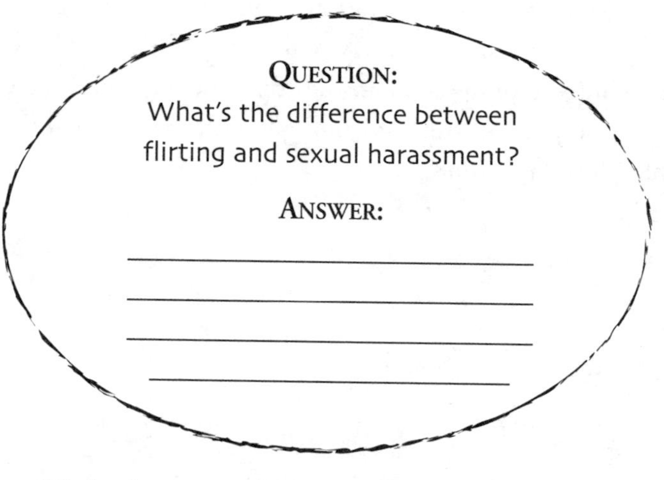

QUESTION:
What's the difference between flirting and sexual harassment?
ANSWER:

(Flirting is two-way and is meant to make you feel good. Unwanted and hurtful remarks, gestures, or actions are forms of sexual harassment.)

Should you talk with your bf/gf/spouse about a sexual abuse/assault that you've had to live through? It all depends. If you feel that it was a big thing in your life, it's probably not a good idea to talk about it with someone you're just hooking up with. I'd make sure I knew the person pretty well and that they'd earned my trust. You have to consider how you would feel if they told someone else. You need to know they will give you the understanding and support you need. Lots of people are ignorant about how abuse/assault happens. Weird as it may sound, they sometimes end up blaming the survivor!

I know these are heavy things to be sitting there reading about — but it's part of life for many people.

Please check out the various places to call or log onto that are listed in the "Still Wondering ... " chapter if you feel confused or upset about this topic. Better still, if there's someone you can trust, go and talk with them. You'll find that you're not alone!

CHAPTER 3

how to ...

(What they never told you in health class ...)

How do you make sure you get the right opening?

— *grade seven student*

My girlfriend and I are going to be married this summer. We haven't had sex yet; what can I do to make sure it's good for her?

— *"Waiting Patiently," male, 20-24*
sexscape.org Web site

As you can see, the range of "how-to" questions I get is pretty big! Those wondering about the basic mechanics of sex are usually younger students. I tell them that there's a reason that genitals don't come with an owner's manual — it's called instinct. As weird as intercourse is — and it is weird — it's also very natural. We are animals, after all!

Back to the above question by Waiting Patiently: asking online is a nice safe way for people to check out things that

they think everybody else already knows. Of course there are loads of other people out there wondering the same thing. Here are some thoughts I passed on to this great-lover-to-be:

As the saying goes, "sex is perfectly natural but seldom naturally perfect." While just poking around is an instinct, being a great lover is an art and takes skill. Same as other skills: some people are just naturally more gifted than others! They're comfortable in their own skin, enjoy touch, can walk the fine line between being relaxed and excited at the same time and, totally important — they're able to connect with their partner. If all these pieces aren't present, are you toast? Absolutely — not! Just because you're not born with huge musical talent doesn't mean you can't play well. You just have to pay attention more and focus on what you do best.

There is no magic formula for a blissful first-time experience. There are, however, some common ingredients shared by those fortunate enough to have an awesome time of it. These include:

- BOTH PEOPLE WANT TO "DO IT."
- THEY'RE FEELING EMOTIONALLY CONNECTED
- THEY'RE CLUED INTO HOW BODIES RESPOND SEXUALLY.

When this is the case, it means that the person is expecting sex and planning for it to happen sooner rather than later. And so, besides having a private place and shaved legs (or whatever), they're also far more likely to use protection.

So, let's look at the awareness piece of this puzzle — Sex 101. I promise that even though this may sound like a "how-to" guide, in the cold light of day (or night), this won't take away from the experience. There's so much that can't be explained about sexual intimacy — that's where the poets and comedians come in! But let's start with some basic knowledge:

1. The most powerful sex organ is

   ____

2. One thing you have to pay attention to if a guy is uncircumcised is ______________

3. If a woman is wet, it means she's ready for intercourse; true or false? ___________

4. Name one of your turn-on spots (besides your genitals):

   ____

5. Four things that make using a condom easier include:

   ____

6. Mark the clitoris with a happy face in the following diagram:

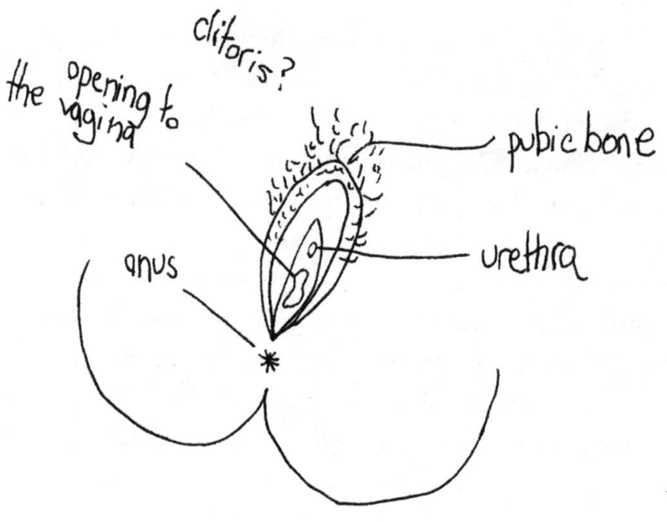

(See answers on page 72.)

Before talking about intercourse, let's remember that sex starts way, way before pants get unzipped. It usually starts with the eyes. That lingering, electric look between two people — yumm. And eye contact continues to be a huge part of the whole sexual play. Voice is also very important for some ... just hearing a message left by someone can make your crotch go "thump." But it's touch that puts us over the top. Brushing past that person at a party. Having your legs just happen to touch when you're sitting together ... zing! *Connecting.* If you savour these delicious moments and understand that sweet sex starts and ends here, then you're laughin'!

People used to use the word "foreplay" to mean everything that happens before intercourse. You can strike that word from your vocabulary — if you haven't already! As one woman says, "it implies that only 'fucking' is really sex or really counts." Guys tend to buy this limited version of "sex" more than females. Unfortunately this approach puts major limits on pleasure, especially for those of us with a clitoris! I hear comments from girls that once intercourse starts, that's it, "it's all we ever do ... we kiss and do stuff only long enough for me to get wet." The making out, hugging and touching are down to a nanosecond.

Quiz Answers:

1. The most powerful sex organ is your brain. Even people who have far less physical ability than others and need to use a wheelchair can experience intense sexual feelings because of the brain's amazing power. And the largest sex organ? Your skin.
2. When you're "uncut" and using a condom, if the foreskin hasn't drawn back over the head of the penis already, you need to gently roll it back before putting on the condom. Also, you have to wash around the head more thoroughly than a guy who doesn't have a foreskin so you don't smell skanky.
3. Not necessarily. She could be making lots of sperm-friendly fertile fluid just because of the time in her

cycle, which means her body is ready to get pregnant, *not* that she's necessarily interested in having sex! Or she could be really horny, but on some meds that make her vagina drier. Or, just before orgasm, often the walls of the vagina make less lubrication than earlier. So, while the vagina does need to be wet for intercourse to happen comfortably, it's a bit more complicated than "she's-wet-so-in-I-go."

4. Hmmm, could be your neck, your nipples (guys or girls), your feet, your inner arm ... you name it! Not sure? It's fun to figure some of this out before having sex with someone — you don't (usually) even have to take your clothes off to find some of your erotic spots.

5. To make a condom easier to use try these ideas.

   a) Practise by yourself first (easier for guys!). Seriously — guys have to get confident coming in one.

   b) Have it close by and slightly opened.

   c) Laugh.

   d) Have more than one in case you goof or go again.

6. Locating the clitoris can be a guessing game for guys and girls. Think of it as being a wishbone or a "Y"; the "legs" extend under the surface and curve around the vaginal opening, with the tip between the opening of the urethra and the outer lips. Pictures are best!

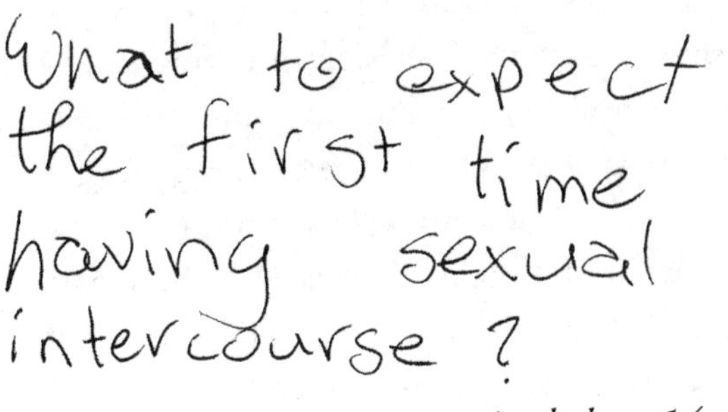

What to expect
the first time
having sexual
intercourse ?

— mixed class, 14–15

If getting off — having an orgasm (that topic's coming soon) — is the only goal someone has, then they should just self-pleasure/jerk off/play with themselves. The kissing, talking, rubbing, licking, holding and squeezing are a world of pleasure that don't always end in orgasm. Being a talented lover has to do with knowing about these delights and wanting to share.

Back to reality: ⇨ how do you avoid the quick kiss-kiss-nibble-nibble-hand-to-crotch-penis-in routine? One suggestion is to do some real serious making-out first, with an agreement that no matter how hot and moist things get, intercourse isn't part of the deal. Think of it as expanding your moves; practising! It also gives you more time to get to know yourself and the person you're with, while sidestepping the possibility of pregnancy and most STIs. Guys who have experienced "blue balls" may groan at this suggestion of just making out, as they remember their aching (but not blue) balls afterwards. Not all guys get "blue balls" to the same degree, and "jerking off" on your own can help relieve the congestion of blood that causes the achiness.

'Blue Balls'

Excuse the terminology, but why does it happen and why do people ie: females not believe men about it?

Communication

(are you listening?)

> Communication is very important throughout sex to avoid things getting uncomfortable.
>
> — *DS, 18*

For sex to be yummy you need to feel comfortable. That means being able to communicate with and talk to the person you're with, especially when you're starting off. For instance, people wonder if they should say it's their first time. My opinion — for sure talk about it! Women who have had the best experiences report that they "shared the fact that they were virgins and therefore allowed their partners to be more physically sensitive."[12] Guys, who often feel pressure to know everything about sex from age three, and don't have the whole pain or blood thing, may not admit that it's their "first." Then they have to fake being cool! It's way better to talk, even in a joking way, about it.

In many of the guys' groups I've taught, there's been discussion of their not-so-great first time experiences resulting from anxiety about penis size, erections, or not "doing it right."

— Anne Barrett, *sexual health educator*

Get used to telling and/or showing your bf/gf/spouse what you like or don't like. Start this kind of openness when you're just kissing or sharing foot massages. You won't find many examples of people being together this way in TV shows or movies, and it's not what gets discussed in schools! In porn you'll hear, "Let me slide my hot ... into your wet ... " But when do we learn to say, "I like it best like this ... ?"

While talking when we make out comes naturally for some, lots of us shut up. We're concentrating on what we're doing. We're shy. We don't want to sound bossy or silly. We don't know if we should be sweet or crude or clinical. Groans and moans go a long way, but as we tell the little kids, "Use your words!" *Everyone* loves to hear how desirable they are and why. And if we don't share the good stuff, it's not easy for the person we're with to hear that, say, washing our ear out with their tongue doesn't do it for us!

How do you approach the opposite sex to wear a condom before having sex.

— teen girls' youth group

Again, being able to talk and listen is a huge part of good sex. I suggest being straightforward. In your most inviting voice just ask, "So, when we get together, will you bring the condoms or should I?" If someone doesn't feel they can freely ask about condom use with the person they're going to bed with ... they probably don't feel they can be open about what they like or if they've really had an orgasm. In that case, you may want to pass on having sex. Also, it's OK to just have condoms with you, no questions asked.

So, you've got the time and place. Protection is covered. You've been making out till you think you're going to die and now you're ready to try that wild thang — *all the way.*

All the Way(s)

Anticipating some action, your body kind of blossoms. There are a ton of changes. Blood gets pumped to the crotch, a guy's penis will go hard (erect), as does the female's clitoris. We don't usually think about women having erections, but they do. Yup, Girls with Boners (good band name)! The vagina gets wet. The amount of wetness is not related to the level of horniness. In fact, at a later stage of excitement, lubrication actually slows down. Vaginal muscles also expand or "balloon out" past the cervix and the uterus pulls up. Nipples become erect (guys and girls) because of the increased muscle tension throughout the body.

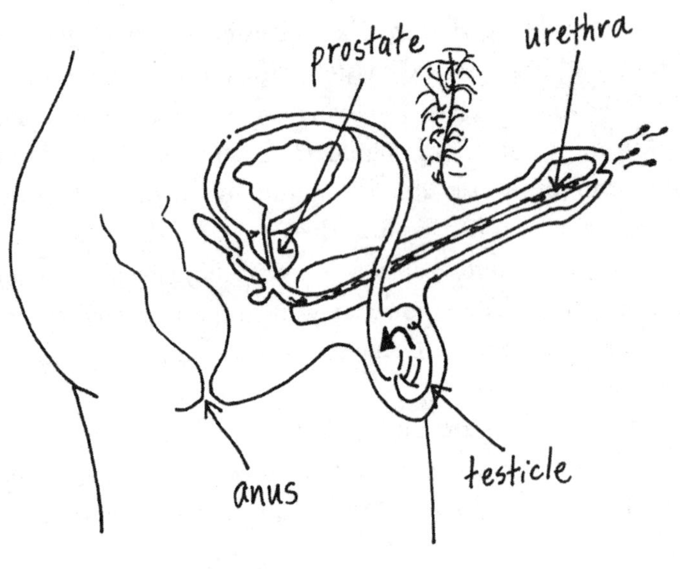

Male Genitals

Slipperiness is a must for any kind of penetration to feel good. If this hasn't happened, then don't try it yet. When a female is tense or scared, nature's lube is not as readily released. Maybe it's your first time, and you're really nervous, but you want to do it anyway. Or maybe you're on meds that dry things up a bit. Depending on the reason for

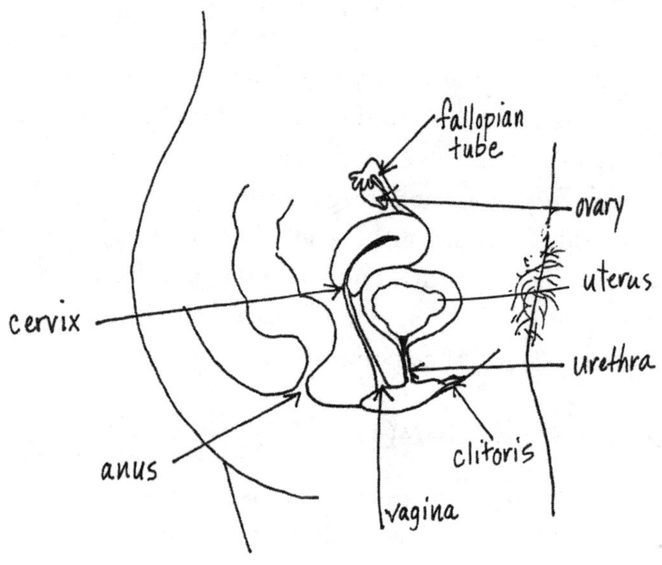

Female Genitals

the dryness, you may need to slow down or add more moisture. Saliva (yours or your partner's) can work well.

Since you'll probably be using condoms (right?!), sex lube, from the condom section of the store, works well along with them. There are lots of kinds to choose from; clinics often give out testers so you can try different kinds. Otherwise, if you're using a polyurethane condom or are "bare-backing" (not a great idea) then petroleum gel or oil (not sunscreen) will do. Having a nice bottle of lube on hand is one of the suggestions from more experienced, fun lovin' women, who have learned that our level of wetness can vary.

Sometimes a guy will stay hard forever. Well, it seems that way. But if a guy's really nervous, or distracted by something (like putting on a condom), his penis may go soft — he'll lose his erection. There are also drugs, such as certain antidepressants, that have this effect on some people. Will he be able to get it up again? Sure, with a little help! Back up, make a joke, take the pressure off. Focus on the things that turn you both on. If he doesn't get hard again that round, you still have your hands, mouth and feet ... you get the point.

Oh, Ohh, Orgasm(s)

For most people, a big part of sex is expecting to have an orgasm or "come." It's what we see in all the movies, right? A couple rocking, gasping, and clutching each other! In reality, especially the first time, guys have orgasms and girls don't. Of the 150 women included in a study, "rarely did [they] actually have an orgasm their first time, even under perfect conditions."[13] What "perfect conditions" meant was that these were young women who were fairly aware of and comfortable with their bodies. We know that as a young woman, you're far more likely to have an orgasm with another person if you've already figured it out on your own before hand.

For you guys, while it's much easier for you to come with someone else, we know that there can be difficulties. Penises not doing what you'd like them to do, mostly because of emotional/mental issues, can be a drag.

Bottom line for both guys and girls? Try to resist the pressure of thinking that this is just all about the big "O." If you can focus on the touching and connecting, you'll be a way better lover and enjoy the experience more.

> How long can a girl's orgasm last? How do females have orgasms in intercourse?
>
> — *grade nine/ten*

No wonder we have such a focus on orgasms. First, unless you're one of those kids who figured this out for yourself at an early age (some start as young as two; it's sort of like thumb-sucking at that point), there's a big mystery around it. Second, people make a big deal about it, in part because having an orgasm has got to be one of the healthiest, least expensive highs going!

There's no rule that says that both people have to come at the same time. Some couples enjoy seeing their partner ride that wave when they're not in the midst of it themselves. Explore, enjoy ...

Physically, we can explain how an orgasm happens. Coming is not that different, physically, between males and females. It has to do with the extra flow of blood to the genitals and the "rhythmic contractions of certain tissues." Exciting, no?

There is in fact the feeling of getting more and more excited and focusing on that arousal. There is the "point of no return" when your body releases the tension. For guys, the moment before the contractions start usually coincides with the "ejaculatory inevitability" or "I'm-coming" feeling. With an orgasm, there's a flood of chemicals released, like endorphins, in both females and males. These leave a person with a wonderfully pleasurable, relaxed feeling after the "climax." For most younger men, orgasm and ejaculation happen at the same time. In fact they are two different things and there are times when one happens without the other, but I won't go into detail about that here.

FAKING ORGASMS. It's something that every female will do at some point, and most of the time a guy will have no idea. Why do we do it? Because we know that some level of excitement is an expected part of love-making; we want to please the person we're with; we've never had the real thing and don't know how to get it; we're tired or sore ... lots of reasons. Faking can become a habit, which robs both the young woman and her partner of full enjoyment. Best not to start. Guys can fake it too, if the lights are low and he's with someone inexperienced. However, it usually takes a while for a guy to lose his erection if he hasn't ejaculated, so it's more obvious what's happening with him.

This is *very important* info that you need to know about female orgasms. While intercourse usually feels good for females, it is not the most common way to get off. Because the clitoris's glans or "head" is away from the vaginal opening, the majority of women need some extra attention to this delicate organ in order to come. This may happen before, during, or after intercourse. It's why stroking and oral sex often get the big thumbs up from women of all ages!

> Can you discuss what guys can do if they experience premature ejaculation ... ? This is a major fear and anxiety factor in young males; it's never discussed in sex-ed class.
>
> — *senior high school class*

There are a couple of reasons some guys come fast. First, when they come by themselves it's like fast food — some quick rubbing and they're done. Also, especially for less experienced males, when they are with someone else, the making-out sensations of touch, taste and smell can be huge. Definitely both people will enjoy it more if he doesn't come the minute he goes in (or before). Suggestions?

- Reduce the pressure and fear by mentioning it to the person you're about to be with.
- Joke about it.
- Come by yourself before you're with the other person, to take the need down a notch.

- Come with the other person, but not through intercourse, and then proceed more slowly.
- Using a condom can slow some guys down.
- You can practise starting and then slowing down very consciously. You can also practise something called the squeeze technique — check out under "Ask Kim" at sexscape.org or in the other Web sites listed in the "Still Wondering … " chapter.

Oral Sex

I haven't seen a study to prove it, but there seems to be lots more oral sex (especially "giving head" or "blow jobs" on guys) than "regular" sex between young people. It's one way that girls avoid intercourse, and most know you can't get pregnant this way. Some feel it's less intimate than kissing on the mouth. People who've only had oral sex still think of themselves as virgins.

(*Are* you still a virgin if you've had oral sex? It's your call ...)

Also, most people know that there is less chance of getting an STI through oral sex. Unfortunately, blow jobs seem like they're just expected now. I'm not saying that there's anything wrong with them — as long as it's not done because of pressure. There is this "double standard" of "what goes for guys doesn't go for girls." Fortunately, there is starting to be more openness around "going down" on a female between guys and girls, which is good for girls, since it's often easier to have an orgasm that way as compared with intercourse!

There is no "right way" to give or get sexual pleasure.

Here are some tips that can be helpful. With oral sex, while you're getting comfortable with it you may want to shower/bathe/swim together first, so you don't have to be self-conscious about stuff like odour. (If you're too shy to bathe together, maybe you need to wait ...)

Start off taking turns — the famous "69" can come later! For oral play on a woman, BE GENTLE. That's the advantage of lips and tongue over hands (or feet). Focus on and around the clit (clitoris); later vaginal play can be added. On a guy, WATCH YOUR TEETH! Females tend to be too gentle. It's advisable to have one hand on the shaft of the penis at the same time that you're using your mouth, both for extra stimulation and so you can control the action, to avoid gagging. Also, there's no rule that says that you have to have semen in your mouth. If you're not comfortable with that part of it, you can either stop before he comes or just say, "don't come in my mouth," and he can pull out.

I get lots of questions about pubic hair and oral sex. (Check out the Q&A in chapter six.) Basically, it's fine to leave the hair and it's fine to get rid of it (if you can handle the stubble of shaving and the pain of waxing!). Do what makes you comfortable. Don't assume in this day of the "Brazilian wax" (totally hairless) that your partner would prefer it all gone; she/he may not.

> Think that vulvas are yucky? The fact is — pussies are cleaner than our mouths ... funky, but clean!!
>
> — TORONTO SEX COLUMNIST *SASHA*

ANAL

Does your butt cum while anal sex? Does your butt bleed the first time you have anal sex?

— *Mixed class, age 14-16*

all the way

I get tons of questions on anal sex from all age groups and genders.

"Doggy" is the position often used for anal or bum sex. For two guys this can be how going "all the way" happens. Lots of people get freaked out at the mention of anal. Partly it's because of homophobia and the misunderstanding that anal sex is only "gay sex." Lots of straight couples engage in anal play. The reason that some people don't see it as "normal" is because it's not how we make babies. Well, you can't make babies by giving or having a blow job either. Also, because it's not often discussed, people don't understand the physical part to it. They believe the "Hershey Highway" is supposed to be only for pooping.

For people who choose to have anal intercourse, it can be very pleasurable. Like all sex, it needs to be a personal choice. There are some young women who choose this kind of sex mainly so they remain "a virgin," or because they don't want to get pregnant. If you or someone you know is in this position, I'd recommend some one-to-one discussion with a hot-line or clinic staff member in order to get more info.

For all people, the anus and surrounding area are sensitive to touch. Basically, the same ingredients for good first time apply here, just as they do with vaginal sex. However, more care is needed for a couple of reasons. First, the area doesn't produce lubrication, so you'll need to visit a store or clinic and get some. Second, the anus doesn't expand as much as a vagina (since it's not where babies come out ...

hope that's not news) and so slowly and gently is the way to go. Best to start with a finger (digital sex!).

Because of these differences and more, **anal sex is the easiest way to get most STDs, including** HIV. Be aware. There can be lots of pressure around this. For a guy having anal sex with a female partner, another word of caution. If you move from the anus to the vagina, you must use a new condom or wash up with soap if you didn't use a condom (not so smart). Nasty bacteria, which live in the bum, can be spread to the vagina, causing infections. And obviously, it's important to avoid any contact between feces (poop) and the mouth!

Positions

What's the best sex positions?

— *Grade 9/10*

As for positions, they're yours to discover! Note — being able to twist up like a pretzel doesn't make you a good lover. I suggest that you not approach this activity as an extreme sport early on in your experience. For a young woman's first time, she may prefer to be on top. Generally, this will give her more control over penetration — the angle, speed and force. In this position, there are more ways for the clitoris to get attention, by rubbing against her partner's pubic bone and/or hands-on play.

Lying down, guy on top ("missionary") leaves entry and rhythm more up to him. He needs to use his arms to support his weight, which means he doesn't have his hands free, or at least only has one of them free. However, his partner's hands are free to enjoy the rest of his body. "Doggy" style has pros and cons. I wouldn't recommend it for the first time, just 'cause it's kind of impersonal. While there is no kissing mouths or nipples, attention can easily be given to breasts and genitals by the person at the back. This direct attention to the clitoris is a huge advantage for that majority of females who do not come just through penis-in-vagina movement.

There are hundreds of positions, literally — standing up, side-to-side, swinging from the trees ... take your time and don't feel like you have to try them all in the first hour!

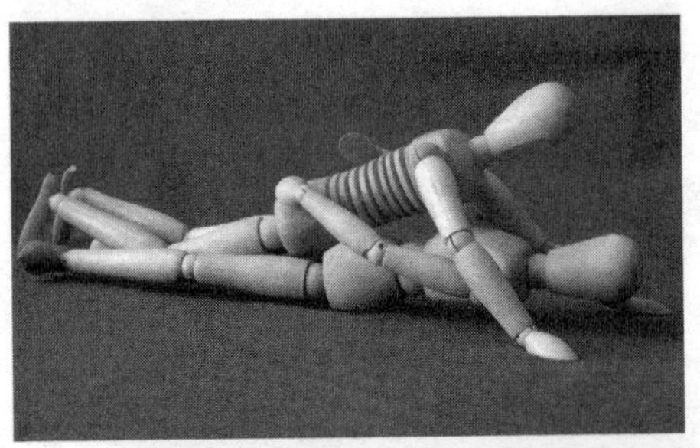

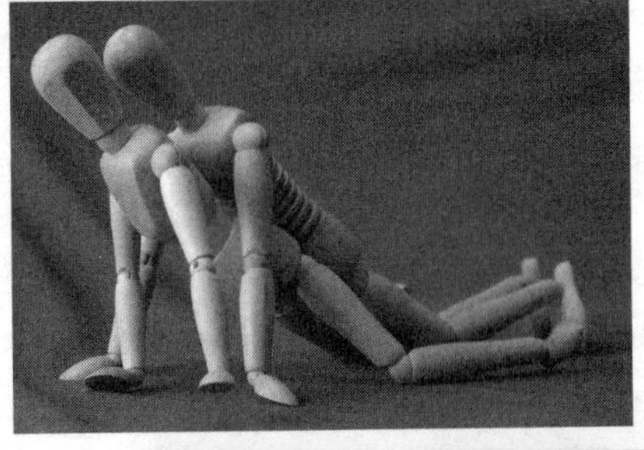

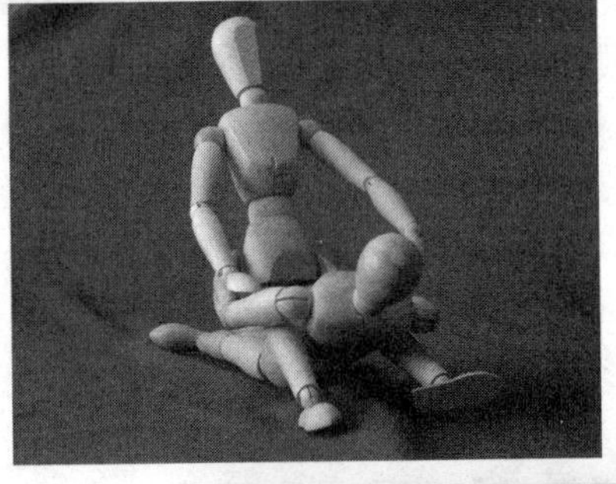

Some positions ...

Hymens

When people think about guy/girl vaginal intercourse, they often wonder about hymens, blood, and all that gory stuff ...

> Do you always bleed the first time?
>
> — *grade nine girls' class*

For the young woman who's never had sex before, my answer is "it depends." Mostly, during consensual intercourse, it will depend on her hymen.

> **The hymen** — a thin membrane that may partly cover the opening of the vagina.

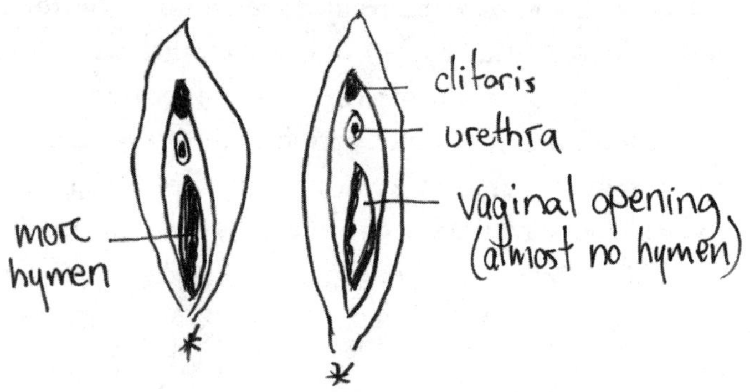

Vulva and Hymen

Just inside the opening of the vagina is the "introitus" (charming), commonly called the hymen or the "cherry." This is a thin membrane of tissue that most girls are born with. It may be thicker or thinner, covering much of the opening or just around the rim. As girls grow, their climbing, cycling, riding and other activity can stretch out this tissue. Later, exploring with their fingers (or their bf/gf's) and inserting tampons further opens up the hymen. Eventually, the hymen becomes "lacy" — nice description, eh?

In the girl whose hymen is just a fringe around the opening, first-time penetration will usually be easy. When the hymen covers more area or is "intact," there will be discomfort and/or bleeding. When I was young, I had a friend who could not use a tampon no matter how much she tried. Her mom took her to the doctor who, after freezing the area, snipped the membrane open. No big deal and it helped her avoid painful first-time intercourse (though I doubt that was her mom or doctor's plan!).

Girls, if you haven't already done so, take a mirror and have a look at your hymen. It's just another part of your body! While you're "down there," you'll discover the clitoris in the folds or "lips" which surround the vulva. Once you know your way around, you can even help stretch out the hymen, and maybe figure out what feels good for you in the process!

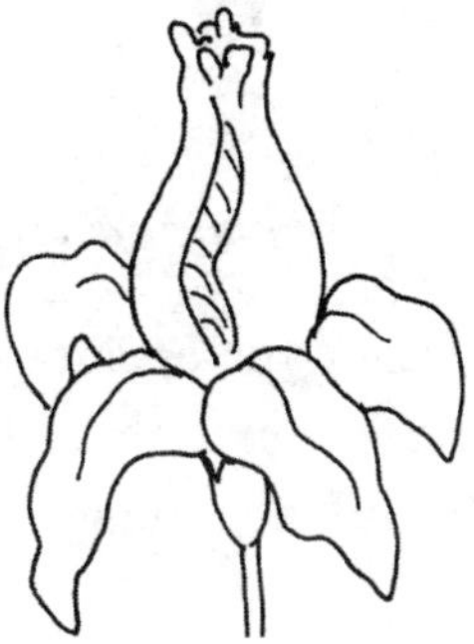

Fingers

When you guys want to make your babe's first time comfortable — get your fingers happenin'! Sometimes people ask about hygiene — besides the usual hand washing, you don't have to worry about vaginas; they aren't sterile! They are nice stretchy little self-cleaning units!

For guys who haven't had much intimate contact, seems that "fingering" (what "base" is that?) is hot stuff. Partially it's 'cause you're finally getting to that juicy secret spot, and also there's this idea that putting things into someone's vagina is automatically a big turn-on. Too many porn images maybe. Two fingers and he's sweating, three and his knees are just about give out. However, since there's often little clitoral contact, for her, it can be a big yawn. To turn up her heat, you need to know what you're doing.

Like I've said before, she's the owner of that amazing body, so check it out with her. You could start by applying pressure to the area at the bottom of the pubic bone, where it curves under, and then say "show me" and move your hand on top of hers. She may not even know what works for her, so you can learn together. Like when you had homework buddies! And all the while, you're helping to stretch out that hymen!

There, that's a quick 'n dirty overview of the physical side of having sex. But we're not just quivering heaps of flesh.

(Yes, yes, everyone feels that way sometimes.) We have the *other* aspects of our selves which are part of this picture as well. There's the psychological or mental part, as well as another less studied aspect, what some call the spirit, the psyche or our connectedness. This non-physical part of connecting with someone sexually is not often talked about, even though it's really powerful. You can have attraction and have all the right moves, but if there's no connection on this other level, then the encounter will feel "flat." Connection is the piece that keeps those couples who stay together happily for a long time wanting more of each other — in spite of gaining weight, annoying habits, and predictable moves!

As you can see, there's lots to know if you both want a sweet encounter. If you've already "been there," don't be shy about sharing some tips with your less experienced friends and siblings as they move closer to going "all the way." True, we're all very different, but there are some pieces of information that are helpful to hear about while you're puttin' it all together!

CHAPTER 4

protecting yourself — from pregnancy and infection

What's the first thing you think of when you hear the word "PROTECTION"?

Pregnancy
Condoms
The Pill
Risk ... ?

Whatever you came up with is probably right — the word somehow fits with sex and protection from pregnancy and sexually transmitted infections/diseases (STI/STDs). No matter who you are or who you're with, having sex comes with risks. Somewhere in your school health classes you've probably covered some of this stuff. Without boring you, I'd like to cover some ways that you can reduce your risks.

> Adults always go on and on about pregnancy and diseases. I've had this for, like, three years now. They think it will scare the crap out of you.
>
> — *grade ten student*

As you know, not everybody uses reliable protection when they first start having sex. A recent Canadian survey showed that 70 percent of teenage females and 81 percent of teen males said they used a condom the last time they had sex. These rates are higher when it's the person's first time (and lower as people get older!).[14] There is also a percentage of teens who use something — like the Pill — that protects them from pregnancy but not from STIs. Most teens know that 1 + 1 = 3 (plus a chance of herpes). They also know something about infections, like, if you don't use a condom you are increasing your chances of catching HIV. So why, knowing these things, would anybody have unprotected sex!? There are lots of reasons, and none of them include the knee-jerk reaction, "because they're stupid."

Health-class movies about unhappy teen moms and pictures of genitals covered in warts may scare students at the time, but we know they don't work well in the long run. What works better is giving straight-up info that really fits the picture for students at that time in their life. As well as info, you need to be able to easily get to a clinic or youth-friendly doctor's office if you decide that you're ready to take the next step in figuring out how to be as safe as possible. And finally, I've found it helps if someone with less experience is given the chance to walk through how the whole safer sex thing can actually work — top to bottom!

It needs to be said that if you're pressured or forced into sex, then it's unlikely any protection will be used. Afterwards, emergency contraception and STI testing can help; they're better than just hoping everything will be OK. But even when both people are into having sex, using protection is not so simple. Slogans like "Cover Me I'm Going In" or "Make It Cleaner, Wrap Your Wiener" are easier said than done. Before taking a look at the different reasons why we end up having unsafe sex, and how to do your best at being well protected, I'll run through some facts about what is available. (Suggestions about how to get access to different kinds of protection can be found in the "Still Wondering ..." chapter.)

This is a huge topic. I'm not going to get into details about all of the different methods and how they all work. There is a comparison chart further on in the chapter. Again, there are some Web sites in the "Still Wondering ..." chapter that can give you loads of detail. What I talk about in class, and will focus on here, are the methods of protection that most people use (or consider using) when they're starting to have sex. Maybe you're with a same-sex partner and so can skip the birth control part of this chapter. However, there are times when queer youth end up with someone of the other sex and suddenly need to rethink the maybe-baby thing.

What's the best kind of birth control?

— *grade ten student*

I get this question a lot, and I hate to say it, but there's no one answer. Lots of educators will say "condoms and the Pill," but you can't give one answer for everybody. Each person/couple has to know the facts (not just what you've heard from ill-informed adults or from friends), and then decide how much risk they are willing to take. Because, as you've heard a hundred times, **the only risk-free method is no penetration, no "sex."** It's unrealistic to say, "don't take the risk" (what, *never* have sex?). We take risks all of our lives, all of us. Some risks come with a higher price, so read carefully before you come to any conclusions.

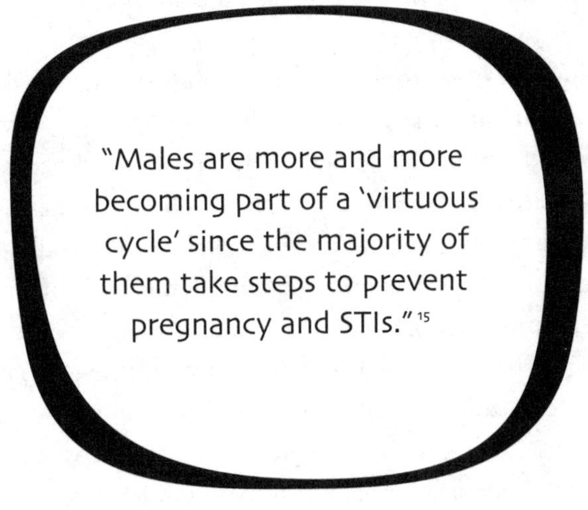

"Males are more and more becoming part of a 'virtuous cycle' since the majority of them take steps to prevent pregnancy and STIs."[15]

Condom — Male

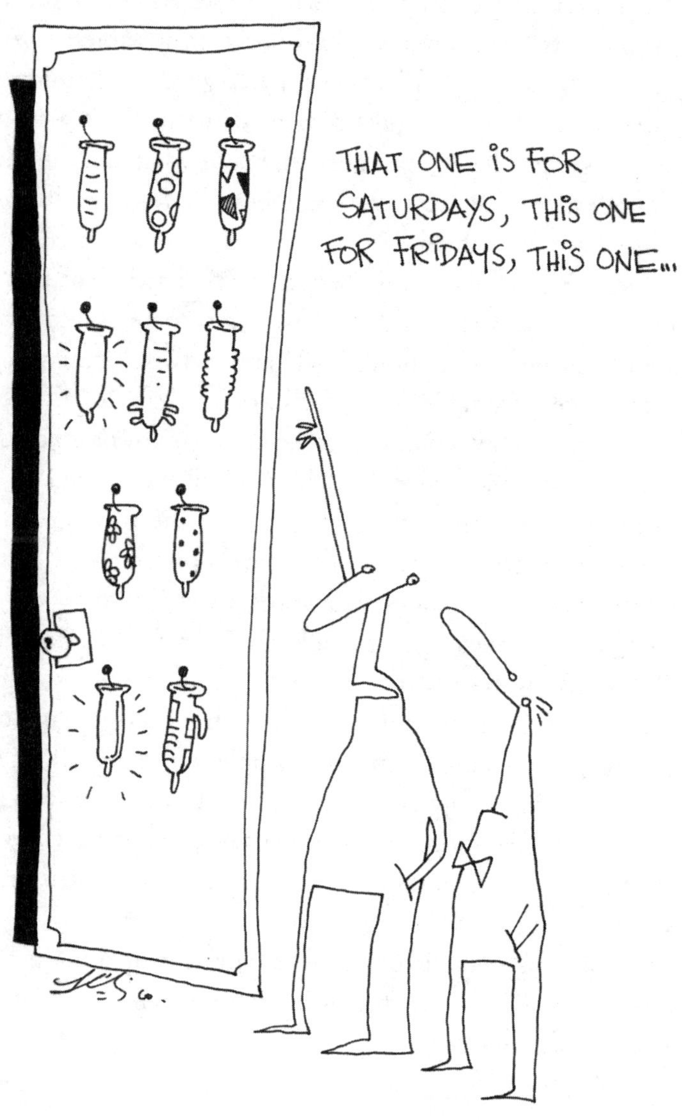

HOW IT WORKS

These charming penis-covers that you see lying around in parking lots and on beaches have some great names: *boner bags, cootie catchers, safes, rubbers, love gloves* ... Condoms work by catching the guy's semen (cum) in the tip so it doesn't go into his sex partner's vagina or whatever. Simple and effective. The more you use them, the fewer problems you'll have with them. Guys, you need to start practising before you're with anyone. Seriously. It's better than practising on a banana in health class. It gives you confidence about getting a condom on easily and lets you know what it feels like to come in one. Also saves on clean up!

As you know, condoms come in a variety of colours, sizes, textures and materials. (See the "Still Wondering … " chapter if you want more info.) Unless the package says "Not for Prophylactic Use," they have all been tested. The standard for testing does change from country to country, so if you're travelling, especially to a developing nation, BYOC (Bring Your Own Condoms). Condoms are usually made of latex rubber, but now come in a polyurethane or plastic variety. This means that people with latex allergies can stop using "Baggies"! (Joking!) People often know they have a latex allergy because their lips react when they blow up balloons or when they have a dentist's glove stuffed into their mouth.

If a guy's penis is quite a bit narrower or quite a bit larger, especially at the base (like the guys in porn), then size can be a problem.

A "thin" or "max" (not labelled as "smaller" or "jumbo") kind of condom may work best.

Don't bother using spermicide condoms. They've never been shown to give more protection and lots of people react to the chemicals in the spermicide — which also taste yucky. (See the section on spermicides below.) Spermicide condoms are not to be confused with lubricated condoms — which I do recommend (especially at first). If you're shy about buying condoms, they can be ordered online or over the phone. Take up stamp collecting or something else that also comes through your mail in a paper package. Honest — the package won't be marked "Condoms"!

HOW YOU USE IT

Number the steps in correct order from 1 to 8 for proper condom use ... (Don't forget to start by having the condom close-by, in a bedside drawer, a pocket, bra, sock ... within reach!)

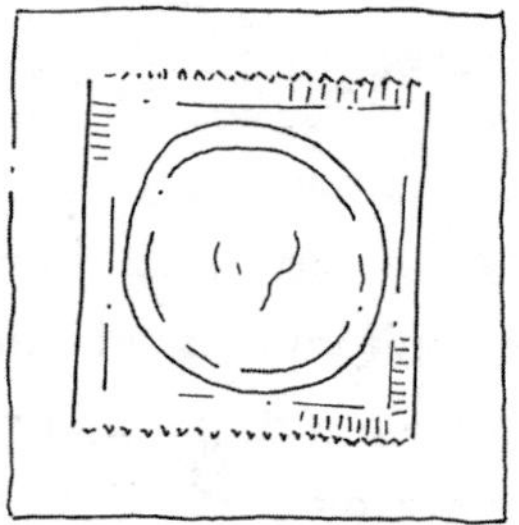

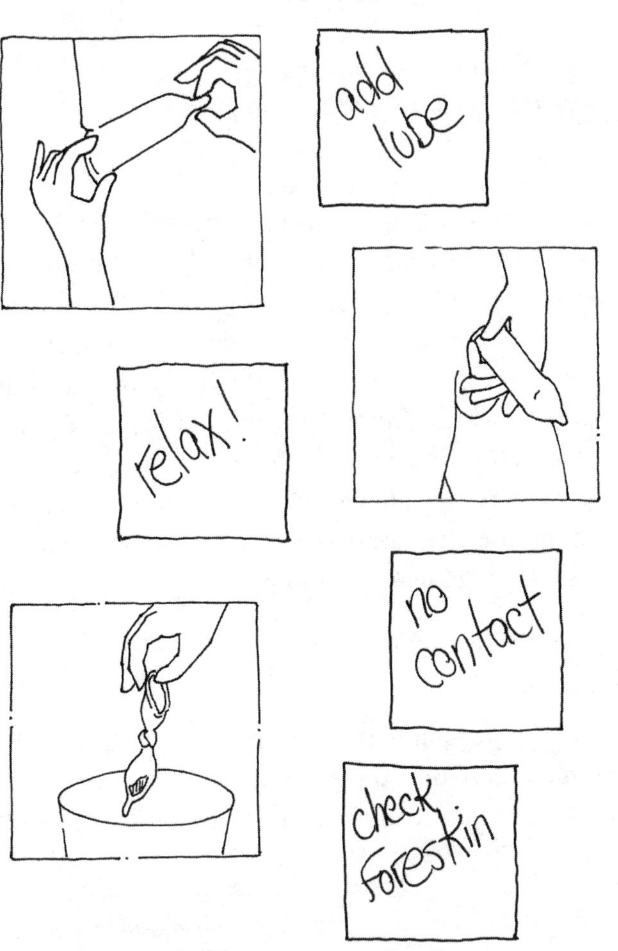

Answer — correct condom use includes:

1. Open condom pouch before things get really hot.
2. Can add a few drops of lube into end to make it nicer for the wearer.

3. If penis has a foreskin, slide it back first (if his erection hasn't done this already).
4. Roll on condom before any contact with vagina/anus/mouth (penis needs to be hard).
5. Pinch the tip so that no air gets trapped in the end.
6. After the guy comes, *hold onto the base* of the condom *before pulling out.*
7. Tie and toss (not in toilet or on the ground please!).
8. Relax & sweet talk!

PROS

If used every time, *condoms work really well.* And, as you've been told and told and told, they are the only things that work well to stop STIs including HIV/AIDS. (There are also female condoms out now.) Because they reduce the sensation on the head of the penis, condoms can help quick-comers slow down. You can even get them with a "slow-down-there-big-guy" cream already in the tip. The different textures and colours can be fun. And there's no wet spot to sleep on afterwards. They make great water balloons. And unlike other methods, this one puts the responsibility in the guy's hands.

CONS

What can I say? If you can't see over the drugstore counter, or you're from a town of five hundred, you may be shy about buying them. So get a twelve-pack from a big store in some other town. Some guys (and girls) make a big fuss about using 'doms. Yup, it "interrupts sex," 'cause you can't put one on too much ahead of time! You'll need to take about an eight- to ten-second break to roll it on. And since it covers the head, it does reduce the sensation there. For some guys, this may mean they have a harder time coming (being really tired or drunk doesn't help). If there's fumbling or anxiety trying to get the condom on, a guy's penis can go soft. This is where practice and a giggle can help. If you're doing it like bunnies, condoms can get expensive. (Buy on sale or from a clinic.) Also, since they only protect the area that's covered, condoms can't give as much protection from STIs such as herpes or HPV (human papilloma virus), which may be outside the covered area.

Because guys control this method, if he's not game, it's a no-go.

In a perfect world, it would be great not to have to use condoms. We could all go "bareback." But as you've probably noticed — it's not a perfect world.

The Pill/Patch

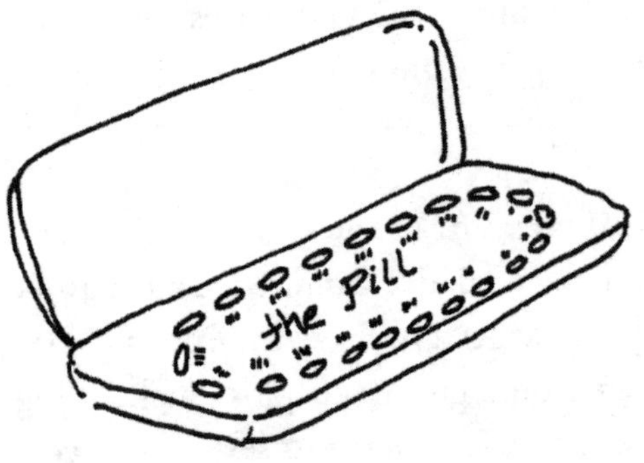

HOW IT WORKS

Mainly, the birth control Pill and the Patch stop ovulation. The egg, or ovum, doesn't get released. No egg, no pregnancy. It also changes the lining in the uterus (so your period is sort of fake) and it thickens the fluid made in the cervix. It does all of these things through the use of artificial hormones. A female's body naturally produces similar hormones, which, during a pregnancy, work more like the Pill.

HOW TO USE IT

You usually have to get the Pill or Patch from a doctor or clinic. Some countries/states allow you to get it right from a drugstore. Wherever you get it from, you should get at least a twenty-minute talk (or more) on how to use it and on the side-effects. There should be written instructions — read them! Even a good health professional forgets to mention important things; I know I have! Often when people decide to have sex, they want it *now!* The Pill/Patch takes at least two weeks to kick in, so a couple needs to stick to kissing and fooling around until it becomes effective.

Basically, with the Pill, you must take it the same time every day. An hour early or late isn't such a big deal. However, missing Pills is the main cause of failure. If you forget a pill for a day, take it and carry on with the pack, but realize that you are not as well protected for the next two weeks or until you get your period. If you're using condoms as well, you don't have much to worry about. If not, you may want to use extra protection such as condoms, withdrawal or spermicide. If you miss two or more pills, you're no longer properly protected — use something else or don't have intercourse until your next period.

Contrary to what you may have heard, the Pill or Patch will not stop you from getting pregnant when you want to. You just stop using it. If your auntie blames the Pill for her infertility, she's mistaken. Maybe she or her guy never were fertile. Maybe she didn't *always* also use condoms, she got an STI such as chlamydia and her tubes (or his) became blocked. There are lots of reasons for infertility, but not the Pill.

> Good news! Two new ways of getting the hormones into you are at hand or close. One is a weekly patch, which works by absorbing the hormones through the skin. It's now for sale in many countries. The other is a ring that circles the cervix and is changed monthly (not as widely available). No more missed pills!

PROS

The Pill is very effective protection against unwanted pregnancy when it's used correctly. The woman has total control over its use. It doesn't "interrupt" sex. There can be some beneficial side-effects, such as regulating the period, reducing cramping and decreasing the chance of some diseases, for instance non-cancerous breast lumps. It usually increases breast size, which can be a benefit, depending on your original cup size!

CONS

Zero protection against STIs — none, *ninguna, aucune, niente* ... Since getting the Pill usually means going to a doctor/clinic, some young women find this a barrier. It may be that they feel very nervous going, or that in some countries/states you actually have to be married or a certain age before you'll be given it (as though *that* would stop someone from having sex!). Some people find it's hard to remember to take the Pill at the same time every day, especially if you're trying to hide the fact that you're taking it. The Patch is easier 'cause you only have to remember to change it once a week.

There are some people who start hormone contraceptives and hardly notice any difference at all in their body. However, there are a bunch of possible side-effects which range from bothersome to dangerous. Nausea, bleeding between periods, increased hunger and therefore increase in weight, and loss of interest in sex are noticed by some. The dangerous stuff has to do with things like blood clots, which you should have explained to you before starting the method. These problems are not common, but you need to know they exist. They are in fact more common during a pregnancy than with use of the Pill!

I've heard that the Pill gives you cancer.

— *grade twelve class*

Have I ever been asked this a lot! There are many studies that have looked at a connection between the Pill and cancer, with the focus being on breast cancer. There are news stories about this all the time. So, what do we know? All of the well done studies conclude that there is no danger. This is still being checked out. If you have worries, it's best to talk to your health-care provider.

My friend said I can't take the Pill because I smoke — is this true?

Many years ago, when very high dose Pills were used, this was the case. As far as the risk goes now: "if you take the Pill and do not smoke, your chances of having a heart attack are actually less than for those who smoke and do not use the Pill."[16] So the real problem is smoking. Of course smoking *and* using the Pill puts you at somewhat higher risk still.

Depo — The Shot

HOW IT WORKS

Depo-Provera is similar to the Pill, except you get the hormone through a needle. The hormone (a progestin), basically stops the egg from being released, thickens the fluid in the cervix and changes the lining in the uterus.

HOW YOU USE IT

Every three months, you need to go to your clinic/doctor and get a needle. If or when you want to get pregnant, you stop taking the shot. It can take many months before your system becomes fertile again, or it can happen right away.

PROS

Since the user doesn't have to remember to take a pill every day, taken regularly, this is an even more effective method than the Pill against pregnancy. It's a very private method, and totally in the female's control. You see the health-care person regularly and can ask further questions once you've started on Depo. There are some beneficial health side-effects (similar to the Pill). Eventually, if you keep using the shot, periods get lighter or disappear totally, which is fine, since there is not a build-up of the menstrual lining.

CONS

As with the Pill, you get no protection from STIs — that's a huge problem. Women who try this method either really like it or really dislike it. The common complaints include "menstrual chaos" (which means you bleed any old time), weight gain and feeling depressed. Once you get a shot, the effects of the hormone last for six months or more (even though the protection is only three months) and so if there is a side-effect you don't like, well, you just have to put up with it. You have to go to a clinic or the doctor's for the shot every three months, which some people find difficult. Bones do not build up the normal density while someone is on Depo, though it seems that this is fixed once the hormone is no longer taken. And finally, needles freak some people.

Withdrawal — Pulling Out

HOW IT WORKS

The guy "pulls out" before he ejaculates ("comes") and so his penis leaves a small puddle of semen elsewhere. Although there *is* a small amount of precum (really spelled "precome") which leaves his body before he comes, contrary to what everybody has been saying (including me until recently), this fluid does not generally contain sperm. It's made in the Cowper's gland, far far from the testicles, where sperm is made.

HOW YOU USE IT

Very carefully. While the "perfect use" effectiveness rate for this method is good, the actual rate, based on what happens in real life, is crappy. If the guy doesn't pull out in time, then there is no protection. Not a pretty picture. And while most guys know what it feels like when they are about to have an orgasm, from practice, they may not get the timing right when they are actually with someone. When he does come, it shouldn't be just outside the opening to the vagina (sperm can swim). Anywhere else is OK — on his lover's thigh, stomach, the ceiling ... wherever. Also, the most dangerous time for pregnancy is during your second romp. If he comes again fairly quickly, then there will be sperm from before waiting in his urethra, which will get flushed into the vagina by the next batch of precum. If he pees between romps, that will "very likely wash the sperm out."[17]

For this method to work effectively, the couple needs to have good communication. And not just, "don't-worry-I-won't-get-you-pregnant." As well, the young woman needs to be able to trust that he will in fact pull out. One person I spoke with said she could recognize when her guy was about to come because "he makes this funny face." There are females who'd rather forget the agreement in the heat of their passion and continue to grind into him on her own way to coming. Or maybe her legs are wrapped about his back ... these things can happen.

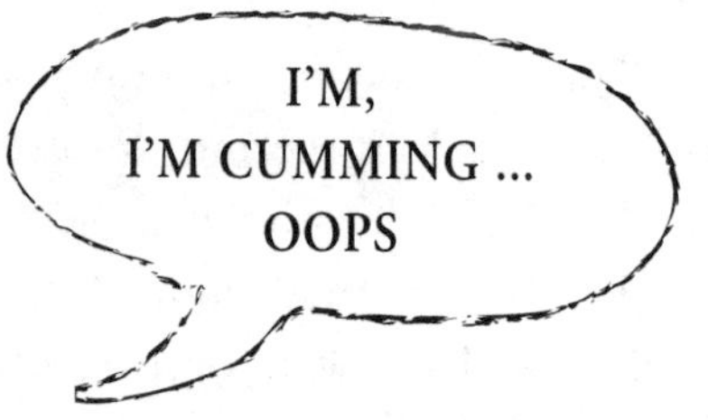

PROS

It's natural, no expense, always available. Can help guys get in touch with what's happening in their body. While still risky for STIs, it can reduce risk somewhat if followed properly, since the amount of exposure to infected fluids is reduced. As we like to say, "It's a great deal better than nothing!"[18]

CONS

Obvious — he has to intercept a very powerful desire to "go deep," and if he fails, his partner is "screwed." The other person may be on the brink of her own orgasm and have that interrupted — which is a major let-down. A minor detail, but his cum can be a bit of a mess. More serious, since we're talking skin-to-skin there's a real risk of STIs. And even if his timing is perfect, the precum and vaginal fluid can have some infection in it and there is zero protection from viruses such as herpes and HPV (human papilloma virus).

> He really wanted me to have his baby, and so he just didn't bother [pulling out].
>
> — *single mother, 17*

Because of all of these cautions, this method is best used with something else — at least spermicide or training in fertility awareness. Some couples who want next to no risk of pregnancy use withdrawal with a condom, in case the condom fails. Couples who have been together longer and who can trust each other can pull this method off with the most success.

Fertility Awareness — or "What's in my underpants?"

HOW IT WORKS

I'm using the term "fertility awareness" (or FA) because it describes women being aware of when they are most easily able to get pregnant, and because, since it's *my* book, I can call it whatever I want to call it! Over and over again when I ask young women "when is the most fertile time of your cycle?", I hear a chorus of confusion. So I ask you — what have you been told? Write it down.

What did you put? — before your period, after or during? By how many days? The easiest and most helpful way of knowing when the egg is about to be released is by paying attention to the fluid (mucus) made by the cervix and found in the vagina. If you understand the science behind fertility, then you can use it both to avoid unwanted pregnancies and to make getting pregnant easier. I've made up a picture on the next page to try to make it easy to remember this info. Hope it helps.

> If you're using any hormone method of birth control (Pill, Patch, Shot ...) then none of this applies, since the ova/eggs are not released and fertile fluid is not produced.

HOW YOU USE IT

Generally females, from the time they hit puberty until menopause (when periods stop), release their egg twelve to fourteen days before they get their period. So even if someone only bleeds every six weeks, the egg will still pop out a couple of weeks before she gets her period. And so how can a woman tell when it's baby-making time, since she can't say

WHEN ARE YOU FERTILE?

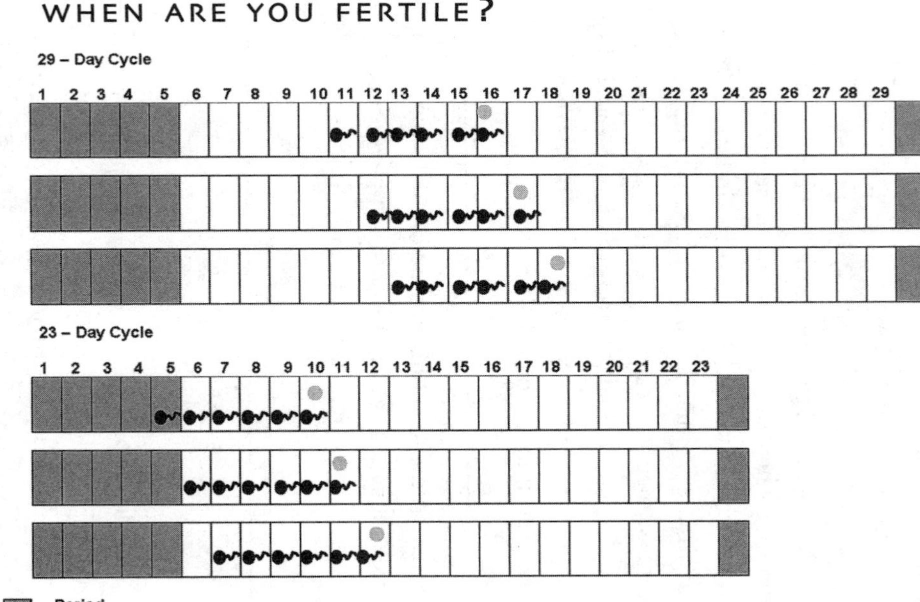

** If you are on Birth Control Pills or Depo-Provera ("The Shot"), this does not apply*

for sure when her period will be? She can pay attention to the fluid or mucus in the vagina. Just how you want to spend your time, right! Here's the story.

To begin with, remember that both the male and female body does everything it can to make a pregnancy happen. It's nature's way, or a conspiracy — however you'd like to look at it! The cervix makes different kinds of fluid depending on the time in the menstrual cycle. About five days before the egg pops out of the ovary, the cervix starts making clear, slippery, sperm-friendly fluid. This fluid starts to be made at this particular time in your cycle because sperm can live for about that long in a female's body, hanging out, waiting for the egg to show up. After the egg is released, it'll only live one day. Then the sperm-friendly stuff isn't needed anymore and so a thick, pasty, cloudy fluid is made instead. This looks like gunk in your undies! Especially dark undies. After another ten to fourteen days, you'll get your period (unless you're pregnant). After your period, a small amount of the thick cloudy stuff is made, until about five days before the egg pops and then ... you got it, the clear fluid starts up again! So, if your period comes about every four weeks, then the riskiest time of getting pregnant is ... *when?*

ANSWER—During the stretchy mucus, seventeen to nineteen days before your period's expected, lasting for almost a week.

I'm going into so much detail here not because this is such a safe method to use but because it's poorly explained almost everywhere else! And I'm only going through the fluid part. The whole FA method involves other body changes such as temperature and ovulation cramps. We lie to youth when we say that "a woman can get pregnant any day of the month." There is only a fertile WINDOW. *However*, knowing when it is can be *very* tricky.

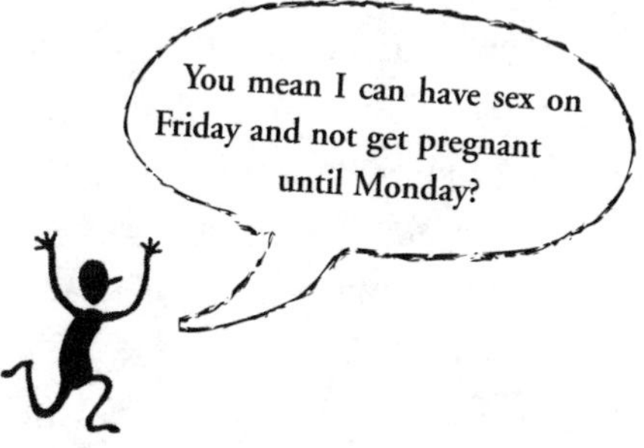

You mean I can have sex on Friday and not get pregnant until Monday?

HOW YOU USE IT

Pay attention to your toilet paper after you pee. Or better yet, slip a finger into the opening of your vagina to test the fluid. Mostly you want to notice how much it stretches between your fingers. Guys can help with this task! "Gross," you say? There are fewer bacteria down there than in your mouth! Now, once you see the stretchy egg-whitey fluid, you know that you are highly fertile for the next week. You have a choice to make. You can avoid intercourse totally or use an effective method like condoms. Let's hope that if there's any chance of STI transmission you'll be using condoms anyway, and FA is just to keep things extra safe. If you're going to have unprotected sex at other times in your cycle, you need *way* more instruction than just this little blurb. This is just the theory. To get the picture for a specific individual takes lots of knowledge.

Some people say they want to use something "natural," and because this method seems so easy, they rely on it as their main method. Or they might use withdrawal. I don't recommend either of these alone, especially for people who are just figuring out how everything works. However, this method used along with any other birth control method (other than the hormones) will help to reduce the chance of a pregnancy.

PROS

Focusing on your fluid is natural, inexpensive, always available. A young woman can get a better awareness of her body, as can her partner. When someone *wants* to get pregnant, they can use this to help increase their chances. Even if somebody's period is irregular, this can help predict when their next one will show up, so they can avoid wearing white that day!

CONS

There's an old joke: "What do you call people who use fertility awareness?"

ANSWER: "Parents." It's true that many couples who only use FA end up with an unintended pregnancy. And, boring as it is to repeat, there is also zero STI protection. It takes discipline for young women to remember to check daily with how things are flowing, and there are several other fluids which can mask the fertile fluid. Long periods, yeast infections, vaginal lube that you make when you're horny as well as semen can confuse the "test." Finally, if this is all a couple uses, then the male partner needs to understand the deal and not push for intercourse during the "fertile" time.

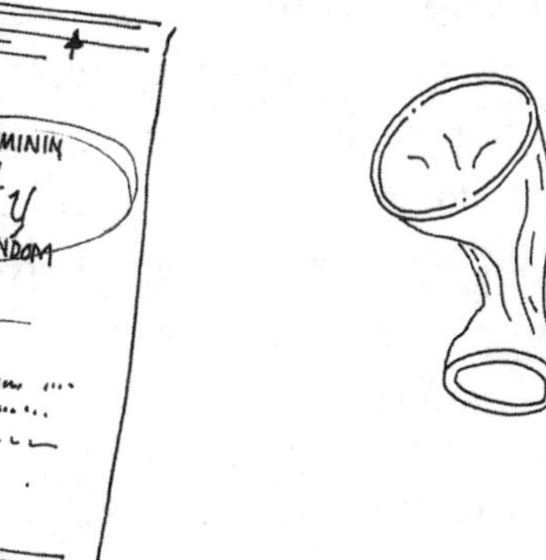

FEMALE CONDOM

HOW IT WORKS

This lubricated polyurethane (fancy name for plastic) pouch fits into the vagina. It stays put by a flexible ring which anchors around the cervix. What stops it from bunching up inside is another ring hanging outside. (See illustration — but only the real thing makes any sense!) Young women either really like these or really hate them!

HOW YOU USE IT

This takes practice. If a girl has been using tampons, then it's probably easier — just knowing her way around down there. Before using the female condom with anyone, insert and remove it at least two times on your own. You'll probably want to wash it off with mild dish soap and re-lube. The inside ring looks huge, but it folds up so it can be slipped inside. Because it shows outside, the guy generally needs to know that this strange and wonderful device is going to be used. He can help put it in (with his fingers, not draped over the end of his penis), but usually women install it by themselves. Once it's in, the tricky part is making sure that the penis slides in the pouch and not up the outside, missing it totally. To remove, just give the outer ring a twist and a tug. Not (yet) reusable, although this is being studied.

PROS

Great protection from pregnancy and STIs if used correctly. Much tougher than the male condom and so it can be made thinner and allow for heat transfer. Size is not an issue. No latex used, so allergies are not a problem. It can be put in hours ahead of time — after you've showered, taken the dog for a walk, talked to your best friend on the phone and gone out to party. OK, not everybody wants to have this Baggie crinkling away down there for hours, but it *is* an option! Also this is the only STI protection the female controls.

CONS

More difficult to use correctly than a regular condom. Some women aren't very comfortable touching themselves. Some people turn off because it extends outside the vagina. Way more expensive than a male condom. You could use it incorrectly and you wouldn't know it.

Spermicide

HOW IT WORKS

You know how pesticides kill pests/bugs? Well, spermicide made of Nonoxynol-9 (N-9) does the same thing to sperm. When it comes into contact with sperm inside the vagina, it kills them. There are many ways of getting spermicide into the vagina. Like hair products, it comes in foams, gels and creams. It also comes in a dissolving film (similar to Listerine mouth-wash tabs) and in a sponge.

HOW YOU USE IT

Spermicide has to be put into the vagina before intercourse. You need to follow the directions. Most types, for instance foam and gels, are put in with a small applicator just before intercourse. The sponge can be put in ahead of time and, like the vaginal contraceptive film (VCF), is inserted with

a finger. You may have heard of the diaphragm, which mainly works by holding spermicide in place against the cervix. (It doesn't block out all the sperm.) Most spermicides melt and trickle out of the vagina eventually. The sponge and diaphragm have to be taken out. There is a newer product called Advantage 24, which is a cream that clings to the sides of the vagina for a day — so you can put it in way ahead of time.

Dealing with 400 million sperm isn't easy, so **using spermicide by itself is not a great idea.** But used with some other protection, it can help.

PROS

Spermicide acts locally, not through the whole body, for just a short period of time. Some, like those used with a diaphragm, can be cheap to use. For most, you can just buy it at the drugstore. It can be used to boost the protection rate of other methods. It is female controlled.

CONS

The chemical (detergent!) causes irritation of the vulva or penis for one in twenty people. If used often (daily), irritation can make it easier for infections such as HIV to enter body. Not a good success rate when it's used on its own. Can taste nasty. Can be messy.

The last-minute kind can interrupt "the mood."

Other Methods

There are a bunch of other kinds of birth control that I'll just mention, but that I'm not going to go into detail with here. Please check the Web sites included in the "Still Wondering ... " chapter for more info.

The IUD or intrauterine device is put in place by a health professional and stays in the uterus for several years. It works quite well to stop pregnancies but increases period bleeding and cramping. It can cause more problems if an STI gets into the vagina. Stays put best in women who've had a kid.

Sterilization, snipping or blocking a man or woman's tubes, is a great method of birth control. However, this is a permanent thing and so is only done once you're older and no longer want to make babies.

The diaphragm and the cap are small reusable firm rubber domes that fit over the cervix. They should be used with spermicide. Not used widely these days.

There are lots of new products to prevent pregnancy and/or STIs that are still being researched. The most exciting are microbicides, which are a fluid or substance that can be put into the vagina or anus to form an "invisible condom."[19] This barrier will then dissolve on its own. I'm often asked, "Is there anything new that a man can use to prevent pregnancy?" Sorry, not even close.

Don't try:

- having sex during a girl's period without any other protection
- using hope or prayer as a method!
- any other crazy things you hear about how to stop a pregnancy

When Plan A fails

So, you used some kind of protection and it didn't work. The condom slipped, she forgot her pills, he didn't pull out ... whatever. It's pretty common, unfortunately. Or you weren't exactly planning on getting that friendly and it "just happened." Worse, you were pressured or forced into sex. **As soon as possible**, talk to a health professional about the emergency contraceptive pills (ECP). This method works well at stopping a pregnancy before it happens! It used to be called the Morning-After pill. This is *not* the "Abortion Pill" that you may have heard about. There may be certain adults who will give you a hard time about getting ECP. They want to punish you for having had sex. They're being ignorant. Every female of reproductive age should have a supply of these in her bathroom. Sometimes you have to go to a doctor or clinic, or you may be able to just go to a drugstore. Here's how it works:

Take it within three days of unprotected sex.
The sooner the better.
You have to take one to two pills and then one to two pills twelve hours later.

THE SOONER THE BETTER.

The only common side-effect is nausea.
There's a new brand out that causes next to no nausea but costs more.
This is not meant to be a regular method of birth control.
(If it's more than three days, go talk to someone anyway; there are other options available.)

BIRTH CONTROL METHODS: COMPARISON

Method	*Failure rate (perfect use)*	*Failure rate (typical use*)*
Nothing/chance	85	85
Promising things to god	85	85
Spermicide only	6	21-26
Pulling out	4	19
Fertility awareness	3	16-21
Condom — female	5	12-15
Condom — male	3	12-14
The Pill/Patch	0.1	3-5
The Shot (Depo)	0.3	0.3

* *This Means You.*

Note that these rates are based on how many women would get pregnant if they used the method for a year. The rates indicate only protection from pregnancy, not from STIs.[20]

Pregnancy

It happens. Most people most of the time try to use something to stop a pregnancy from happening when they make love. But nothing works all of the time. So a young woman may miss her period or have an unusual one. She may (or may not) start to feel tired, hungry and a bit barfy. Something makes her get a pregnancy test.

If it's a positive test, she has three options. Depending on her country, culture, age and family, she'll be more likely to choose one option over the others. **There is no easy choice.** If she goes ahead with the pregnancy, let's hope she will get good care that will help her have a healthy baby. She may keep the baby or give it up for adoption.

> Beware: People who don't believe that abortion should be a woman's choice set up biased pregnancy counselling services. They delay giving out results, give out false information and do not offer information on the full range of options.

She may decide that she does not want to have a baby at all. Ending a pregnancy is called a "therapeutic abortion" (or TA). I'm going to explain more about this choice since it's the one many young women choose, and it's often skipped over by educators and parents for political reasons. A poor excuse for withholding information.

As you're aware, there are many different feelings about abortion. People growing up have to decide for themselves, although my wish would be that nobody would ever have to be in this position in the first place. But that's not going to happen in either of our lifetimes! There are also many different laws about this option. In Canada, it is up to the young woman to decide. If she's a teen, after talking with a doctor or counsellor, she's usually encouraged to let her parents/guardian know what's happening. But she doesn't have to. Almost all abortions are done within the first twelve weeks. The TA is covered by the health care system. England has a similar system.

In the USA, it depends on which state you live in, with some being more like Canada and some banning TAs. Whenever choices are limited like this, it doesn't stop women from seeking abortions: they just do it illegally. This is dangerous to their health and expensive. Having a (legal) abortion is much safer than having a baby, and it won't interfere with future pregnancies. Emotionally, most women (some guys too) will feel a mixture of relief and sadness afterwards. If they get good service, it will include counselling regarding how to try to avoid getting into the same situation again, although unwanted pregnancies can happen more than once.

Heavy decision, eh? If you're going to have sex with the opposite gender, you have to be prepared to deal with this, because there is no 100 percent sure way to stop a pregnancy from happening. Best to know what the person you're with would want to do if a pregnancy did happen.

Just fooling around together won't take you down this road — so if you're not ready to take the risk ...

Of course, if you make love with someone of the same sex you don't have to worry about pregnancy, but you still have to deal with the possibility of STIs. That's what the next chapter covers, so whether you're straight or LGBTTQI (lesbian, gay, bi, trans, Two-Spirit, queer, intersexed), read on!!

HOW YOU REALLY, REALLY MAKE SURE YOU USE THE PROTECTION YOU WANT!

Or, how can you cover your ass, knowing what you now know?

So, now you know all these facts about protection. Many people I've seen in clinic are well informed, but they still get into problems. They still end up with chlamydia or pregnant. It's like, we know lots about how to eat to stay healthy and fit, but we don't always do it. We're not robots. There's lots of other stuff going on which affects our actual choices.

To begin with, you have to decide how much or little risk *you* are willing to take. If you say "none," well then stay in bed, 'cause Life is Risky. Actually, with this issue, you'll have to stay out of bed! Really, right now how much risk are you willing to take? To put it down in black and white, plot your decisions on the following scale:

PREGNANCY (BEING OR GETTING SOMEONE ...):

0 1 2 3 4 5 6 7 8 9 10

no risk some risk whatever

SEXUALLY TRANSMITTED INFECTIONS:

0 1 2 3 4 5 6 7 8 9 10

no risk some risk whatever

If you scored 0 on both, unless you're planning to do it with somebody from another planet, you'd better think again. There is no such thing as no risk when it comes to sex. Even between two people who say they're virgins.

If you scored from 1–5, then you have enough good reasons to want to play safe. Checking out the comments below will help you follow through.

If you scored from 6–10, depending on who you end up having sex with and how often, you'll fish your wish. Pregnancy and infections come easily to those who use only so-so protection. If your main focus is pregnancy, because you don't think you have to worry about STIs, a hormone method (Pill or Depo) will work well. But don't kid yourself about the STI factor. Even a steady bf/gf/spouse may end up sleeping with somebody else.

OK, so now you've been clear with yourself about what you want. What could possibly get in the way?!

Passion.

Pressure.

A couple of drinks.

Feeling you're in love.

They say they've been tested.

Not wanting to look like a wuss.

You didn't quite make it to the clinic.

It feels too embarrassing to say anything.

The condoms are in your drawer ... at home.

It was only one Pill you missed ... and one last week.

A voice in your head whispers to you, "swept away is OK."

You are in the "what's meant to happen ... " state of mind.

A mountain of reasons!! And there are at least another ten pages I could have added! By the way, this list doesn't just apply to young people, this is for everybody. What you need to do is give yourself some time, before the event, to think about what is likely to get in the way of your using protection. When you take driving lessons, it's the same thing. You spend lots of time learning about all the possible ways accidents can happen in order to be able to react quickly when you're actually in the situation. You learn about slippery roads, people who will cut you off, drinking and driving ... The best way to avoid the "accident" is to be able to see it "cumming" and do something about it!

So, given what you know about yourself and about the person you think you'll be with (if you have any idea yet), be real about what's most likely to get in the way. What's gotten in your way before, in a non-sexual setting? Like, when you need to study and someone calls and settles into a long blab, what do you say (if anything)? Or how have you dealt with stealing or a fight? Was it easy for you not to get involved, to be assertive? Are you the kind of person who goes along with things so there's no conflict with your friends? Are you most likely to give in, or to get your way? Well, it won't be that much different with sex stuff.

Here are some questions that may help you see an "accident" before it happens.

1. From *inside* yourself, what's most likely to stop you from using the protection you plan to use? (For example, shyness, not wanting to look "prepared," religious teachings, inexperience, having a desperate need to please the other person, getting off on risky stuff ...)

2. What are the things *outside* yourself that are most likely to stop you from using protection? (The person you're wanting to be with doesn't want to use anything, not easy to get to a clinic, money, friends don't use condoms ...)

3. When, where and how can you picture talking about protection with the about-to-be-lucky person? What would you actually say? Would you mention protection the first time that having sex comes up? Would you just plan to have a condom with you? What's your plan ... ?

It's tempting to just think, "I'll deal with this when the time's right," but, honestly, that can be an excuse for avoiding a potentially awkward talk. My advice — put it out there early on, not once you're lying together naked!

"Regardless of how you do it, I hope you can attain open communication with your partner. It has been my experience and that of many others I know, that communicative sex = more enjoyable, safer sex. Good luck and have fun!"

— Annie Grainger, teen writer, *The Little Black Book*[21]

Just like when you're driving a car or a bike — if you could actually see the accident before it happened, life would be so easy! It's because things always happen fast that they take us by surprise. But there are also bad driving habits that new drivers get into that make accidents more likely to happen. Drive too fast or skip WEARING A SEAT BELT and you're way more likely to end up dead in a ditch ... or getting banged up. We also don't have any idea how powerful a feeling or desire is before it happens. All we can do is be as prepared as possible, which means not living with our heads stuck up ... in a cloud.

CHAPTER 5

infections — sexually transmitted infections or diseases (STIs or STDs) and other gross stuff

How many people do you know who've had an unwanted pregnancy or a scare?

None ☐
One ☐
Lots ☐

How many people do you know who've had an STI/STD or gone for testing?

None ☐
One ☐
Lots ☐

Most straight couples who sleep together worry more about an accidental pregnancy than about sexually transmitted infections or diseases (STI/STDs). This is partially because by their mid-teens, most people (especially girls) know someone who's had a pregnancy scare. Seldom do we hear that "so-and-so" has a case of some yucky disease they got through sex. Well, "so-and-so" may have picked up an STI, but it's not the kind of thing they'd blab about. Unlike a pregnancy, there's no drama or positive attention to be had. You keep very quiet about it. The exception to this is that after a presentation on AIDS, we sometimes get a bunch of friends who come together to the teen clinic and get tested — but I don't think any of them actually thinks they'll get a positive test back.

So we don't usually hear about it when people get hit with an STI. Later on, couples who can't make babies don't go around explaining how PID (pelvic inflammatory disease) made them infertile, or wearing T-shirts that say, "I've had an STI."

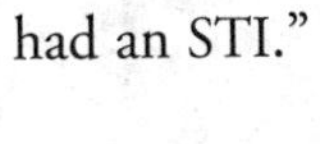

OK, there are lots of other reasons for infertility — but in many cases it's connected back to an STI either not treated at all or not soon enough. It's just like people with HIV; they don't generally advertise the fact that they're positive. We don't like other people judging us, especially on very personal matters. So with all this silence about these very common diseases — nobody believes they are lurking close by. It's like that scary thing you used to think was under your bed, but now it's real and in bed *with* you!

You've already been taught the basic facts about HIV and some other sexually transmitted infections or STIs, right? Adults love to spend most of your sex-ed time on this subject because we think it will scare youth into not having sex — ever. Just look around to see how well this approach works! So, what do you really need to know? Not *all* the symptoms for *all* STIs and *all* their treatments. For that kind of detail there are sources listed in the "Still Wondering ... " chapter. Here, I'll cover what you are most likely to run into, how you might know you've picked up something, getting tested, and what can or can't be done about it. Of course I'll hit you over the head again with how to try to avoid infections.

> If neither my girlfriend or I have ever had sex before, why do we have to worry about STIs?
>
> — *clinic client*

Good question. And there are at least two good answers. First, it has to do with *never* knowing 100 percent that the person you're going to be with is "clean." If young people have been forced to do unwanted sexual things, or did them for money or drugs, they'll block out this past and usually not discuss it. Also, there are ways of catching viruses such as Hep B and HIV other than through sex.

Second — I encourage people to use condoms RIGHT FROM THE START, just as part of sex play. Think about it the same way as wearing a decent pair of runners for sports. You wouldn't step onto the court or field with leather-bottomed shoes or high heels. At some point, you know you'd get hurt. Condoms need to be a habit, an automatic thing, part of the equipment. For guys especially, it's easier to start off covered rather than at some point deciding to cover up. You're used to the feel of it. Also, if you break up with your "first," then when do you start with the safer sex? After your second gf/bf? Third? Only with strangers? Remember, by the time they finish college or university, many people have had at least ten partners. If you're going to do it, do it right from the beginning.

bf/gf = boyfriend/girlfriend

Here's a quiz of twelve commonly asked questions that can help you check out what you know:

1. What exactly are STIs?
2. How would you know if you (or another person) had an STI?
3. Is oral sex safe? Explain.
4. What's the difference between cold sores and herpes?

5. What STI is a young woman (age 15–21) most likely to need treatment for?
6. Why is it important for females to get a Pap test at least once a year?
7. How soon after possible exposure can you get an HIV test? Is there an AIDS test?
8. Why is anal sex the riskiest?
9. Can some infections get through condoms?
10. Why is it recommended that all pregnant women be offered an HIV test?
11. Does size matter? (Size of condom ...)
12. What do you know about yeast infections?

ANSWERS:

1. As the name says, these are infections that can be passed between sexually active people who have at least some of their clothes off from the waist down. We usually talk about "penetration," which includes oral and anal sex. There are two main kinds of infections — bacterial and viral. If a person knows they have one of the bacterial kind, such as chlamydia, gonorrhea or gardnerella (pee-yeew), then they can get medication and be cured. If somebody gets one of the viruses, medicine *can't* cure them. The viruses are the 4-H Club:

Herpes
HPV (human papilloma virus)
Hepatitis B & C
HIV (human immunodeficiency virus)

2. The problem with lots of STIs is that often there are no signs or symptoms. Your private parts don't turn green and fall off. You don't end up sick in bed for days (right away at least). For yourself, with the bacterial infections (chlamydia, syphilis ...), if you're lucky you may notice something unusual anywhere from two days to four weeks after unprotected sex.

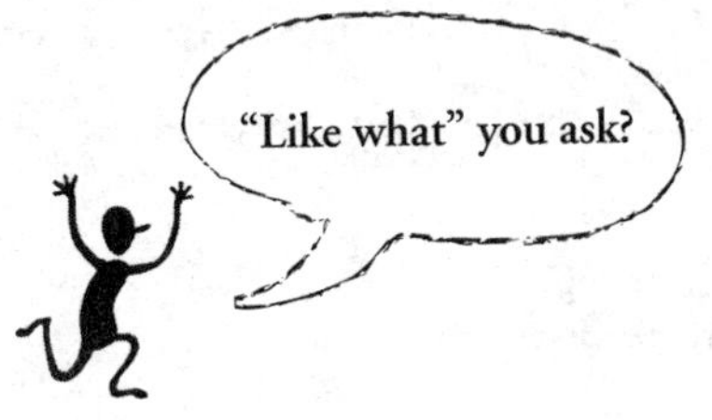

You may get a burning feeling when you pee, an unusual discharge from the penis or vagina, an irritation or sore on the vulva or penis, painful intercourse, or bleeding during sex.

If left untreated, these can become a very serious condition called "pelvic inflammatory disease" (or PID), which can leave girls hospitalized and/or unable to have kids. Syphilis can cause a painless sore where it enters the body (genitals, cervix, anus ...) which disappears as the infection is carried in the bloodstream to infect other parts of the body, damaging this and that at it goes

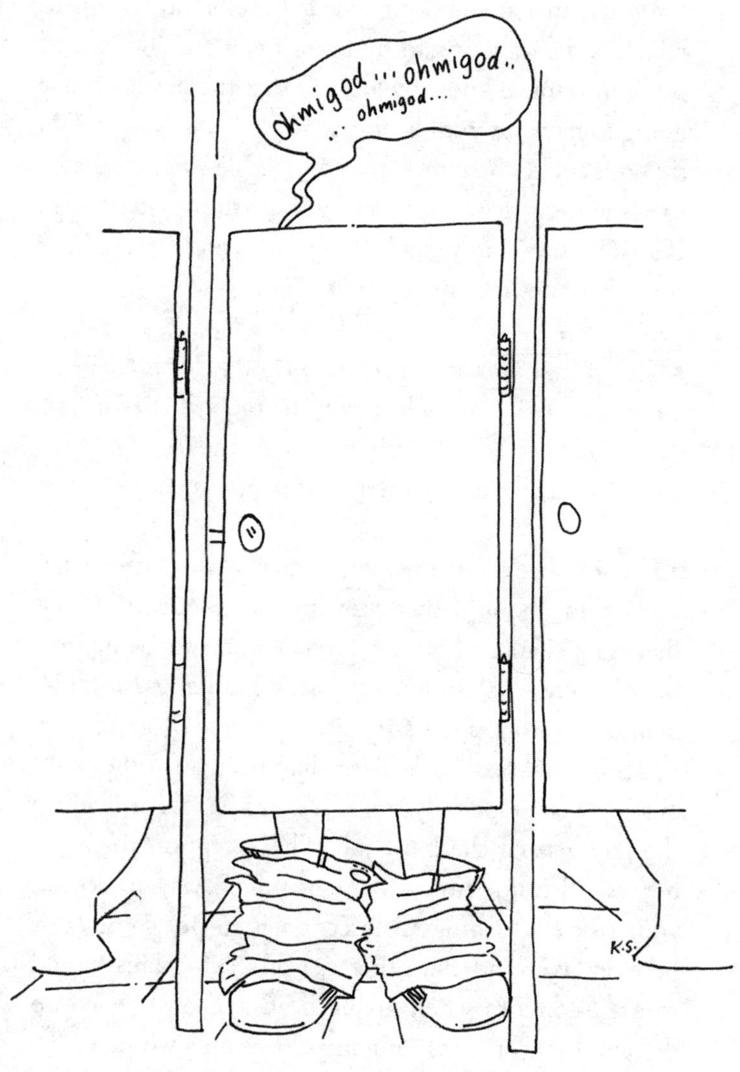
ohmigod ... ohmigod..
... ohmigod...
K.S.

merrily along. With HIV you may look and feel just fine for years, and so you don't even get the blood test for it, which is the only way to find out if you are infected.

If you want to know by looking that the person you're going to have sex with is disease-free — *you can't.* Again, if you're lucky there may be a noticeable sore, discharge or something weird, but usually these things go unseen. If anyone says they've had all their tests and checked out fine, that doesn't help you because ...

- Clinics and doctors don't routinely test for *all* STIs.
- Healthy results go right down the toilet if they have any unprotected sex, even once, after the tests (and you wouldn't believe how often that happens ...).

3. Oral sex won't get anyone pregnant (no matter what we're told about babies growing in "tummies!"), but there is a chance of getting an STI when someone puts their mouth on somebody else's genitals. Although many educators don't say this, your risk of getting an STI from oral sex is way lower than from any other kind of sex. This is especially true if it's on a female or if you're the guy getting the blow job. The exception to this is herpes. (See question # 4 below.) The way to reduce your risk of catching an infection is to put some latex between you and the other person's skin. This would mean a condom when giving head and an opened-up dry condom (or dam) for going down on a women. The other risk reducers are:

- Make sure you don't have any sores in your mouth, throat, gums ...
- Tell your partner not to come in your mouth.
- If anything comes your way, spit (politely of course).

4. The main difference between cold sores and herpes are their location. They are caused by a similar virus, HSVI or HSVII. The blisters caused by this virus usually appear on mouth or genitals. The viruses can be passed from mouth to genitals and vice versa. This does *not* mean that your math teacher who has cold sores got them from oral sex ... or it's highly unlikely. Casual contact when you're younger, such as sharing a drink or lip gloss, can give you cold sores.

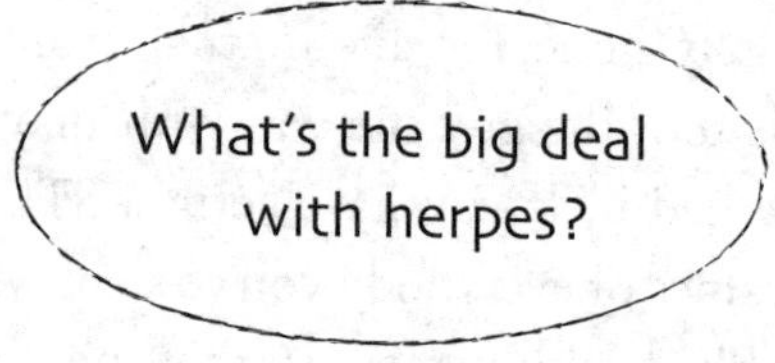

What's the big deal
with herpes?

Well, apart from having to tell your future partner(s), the most dangerous thing is the possible transmission of herpes from a pregnant woman to her baby. This can lead to permanent brain/nerve damage or death.

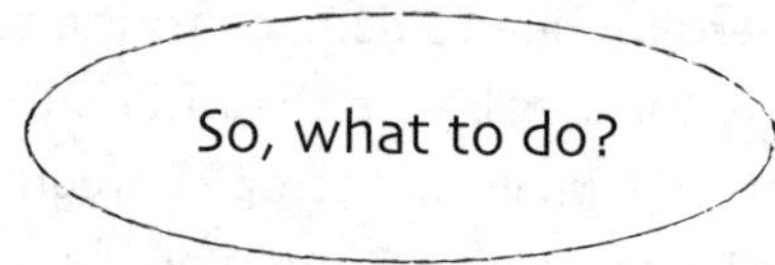

So, what to do?

Don't assume that you can just go down with a flashlight

and check out the person you're with (one guy I heard about loved this activity). The herpes sores may be inside the vagina or urethra and not noticeable at all. People "shedding" it without having any symptoms or obvious sores can also spread the virus. "Shedding" is when some of the virus is released without an obvious blister. Again, if you choose to have intercourse, condoms are your best option. Of course they only protect what's covered ...

5. If you answered that "chlamydia" is the STI that many young women get treated for, then you're right (or you read this already and cheated). While it's really common, 80 percent of the time females won't know they have it. So how do people find out and get treated? If they don't get any symptoms listed above in answer # 2, then maybe they've wisely gone for an internal exam. Or, since guys get this too, the guy she was with may have found out that he had it. If you have certain STIs, you need to give the names of everybody you've slept with to your doctor or public health person, so that they can be contacted and get treated.

   What if you're unlucky and don't know that you have chlamydia? Worse case is that you end up in the hospital with pelvic inflammatory disease (PID), which is a major cause of infertility due to damage to the tubes. You may not able to make babies in the future. Or you may end up with a "tubal" or ectopic pregnancy. Infertility due to STIs can happen to either sex. A less common STI, gonorrhea, can have the same effect.

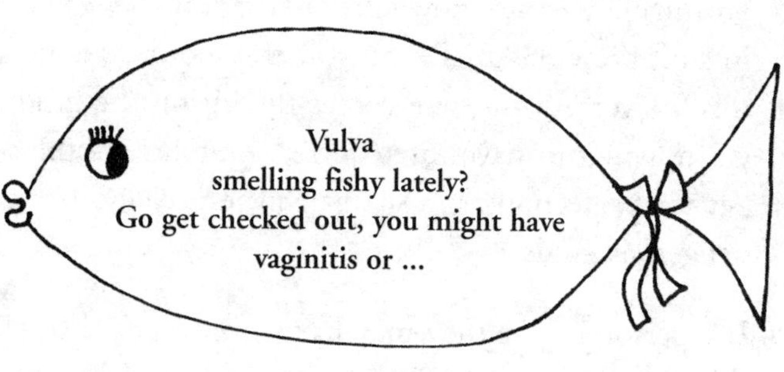

Vulva
smelling fishy lately?
Go get checked out, you might have
vaginitis or ...

6. The only way a female can routinely get tested for problems caused by likely the most common STI is through a Pap test. The infection is called HPV or human papilloma virus. (One type of these used to be called genital warts.) There's no cure once you get it. I say "likely" the most common because this is not one of the infections we keep track of and because you can have it for a while but not know it. It's spread by skin-to-skin contact, though not very easily through oral sex.

   The main problem happens if a female gets a certain kind of HPV (there are about twenty-five of them) on her cervix. And how the heck would she know if she had such a thing on her cervix? Through her regular Pap or internal exam! If left untreated, the abnormal cell changes caused by the virus can result in a high risk of cancer of the cervix. If detected early on, treatment is fairly simple and very successful. The HPV types that look like warts (you can see/feel them), can be taken off at a doctor's office. These are not the dangerous kind.

Fortunately, we also now know that our bodies can often toss off the virus totally. So you may not be stuck with this forever. Again (here comes the hit on the head), if you're going to have intercourse, condoms are the best bet for protection against this STI, especially the most dangerous kinds.

7. If a person thinks they may have been exposed to HIV, the virus that causes AIDS, they need to stop having sex or use condoms carefully, and wait about twelve weeks to get a blood test done. The same goes for people who have shared needles, which is a really easy way to get the virus. As you know, the virus is passed through body fluids, mostly blood, cum and vaginal fluid. Kissing and casual contact don't spread this virus.

   There are hot-lines listed in the "Still Wondering …" chapter — the people who work at these hot-lines can answer specific questions you may have about HIV and risks. There isn't an AIDS test, because AIDS isn't an infection. Doctors diagnose someone who is HIV positive as having AIDS when their immune system is wretched because of the virus. A really important part of their immune system, T4 or helper cells in the blood, goes way down. And the person ends up having one (or more) of the life-threatening illnesses common to this disease.

8. Anal or bum sex is the riskiest for infections because of how the anus is made. First, it's not as stretchy as a vagina or mouth. It's not self-lubricating, and the blood

flow is closer to the surface. To be safer, anal sex has to happen more gradually, with lube, and with the "bottom" (or owner of the bum) able to relax. Otherwise, tearing can happen and bump up the chance of STI transmission. And all bums are the same — regardless of gender or orientation. See the "How To ... " chapter for more info.

9. STI cooties cannot get through condoms. Latex and polyurethane 'doms are tough. Natural skins, used from sheep gut, are more porous and way more expensive, so don't buy them. No, when condoms fail it's mostly incorrect use or a size problem. Sometimes they split or slip off. The guy usually feels when this happens. We know condoms work well because when one person has an STI and uses them correctly, their partner rarely ends up with the infection. See page 101 for correct condom use.

10. It's *really* important for all pregnant women to get tested for HIV for the health of the baby. If someone is pregnant, unless they got that way through medical assistance, it means that they've had unprotected sex. And that means that there is always the chance, however small, that she could have caught the HIV virus. If we know a pregnant woman has HIV, then we can give her medication to SERIOUSLY REDUCE the chance that her unborn child will get it ... good news! The chances that the HIV virus will be transmitted from the mother to the fetus drop from 15–30% with no treatment to 1–2 % with treatment.[22]

11. Does the size (of condoms) matter? Sure. For years I said one size fits all — which is like saying all women can wear the same size stretch bra. We probably could, but for some it would bust at the seams and for others it would hang down around our ribs. Penises are generally an average size, as are condoms. However, there are some guys who are narrower at the base, or much bigger, and so condoms may either slip off more easily or split. Fortunately, now there are condoms made in different widths and lengths. Condom stores and online shopping make buying them even easier!

12. Yeast infections happen for lots of different reasons. Women mostly get yeast infections from something that throws off the normal yeast balance in the vagina, such as taking antibiotics or being on the Pill. Damp non-cotton bathing suits and undies don't help. Also, the infection can be passed on by a guy. If he gets an itchy burny feeling around the head of the penis, and hasn't always been using condoms, it may be a yeast infection he picked up during sex. And then he can pass it back to his partner, like ping-pong, or to a new partner. While yeast infections aren't really considered an STI, they can be transmitted that way. So both people need to be treated.

    If you've had intercourse, and it's the first time you think you have a yeast infection, go get it checked out before taking anything for it, just to make sure that's what it is.

It's important to treat any problems, including yeast infections, because the white blood cells, which are made to fight off any infection, can also let HIV pass more easily through the wall of the vagina or urethra.

THE BIG MISTAKE

Some people think that they can avoid getting a STI by knowing the person they sleep with. As long as they seem cool and you know where they're from and who they hang with, they're probably, you know, not infected. Think again! As you've just read, people often don't even know they are infected with something. And people often lie about sex stuff … They're not honest about what they've done with whom, when, and what protection was (not) used. They do it to cover up embarrassing things and to make you feel more comfortable. SO DON'T EVEN ASK! Or if you do, don't count on a totally honest answer. If you're serious about wanting to avoid getting infected — use condoms every time.

How'd you score on that quiz? Obviously there's a ton more to learn, so keep your eyes and ears open for new stuff on this topic. After you've got the facts, the really tricky (sticky?) part is using what you know. Most people know about HIV, and that there are other STIs, but many don't use a condom every time they hook up with someone. What would stop you from protecting yourself? You can check out more about this in the "Protecting Yourself" chapter. Basically, having sex without using a condom is like playing with fire — you will get burned if you keep doing it. It may be just a scorch on your finger or it may be third-degree damage to you or someone else. Play safe.

CHAPTER 6

will it, like, hurt?

In the classroom, in clinic, on call-in shows and online I get flooded with questions and situations about sex. In class, these are often anonymous written questions and so, while I know the age group, I don't actually know anything else about the person. The questions that follow are all real questions. I've chosen some common ones that you also may have wondered about.

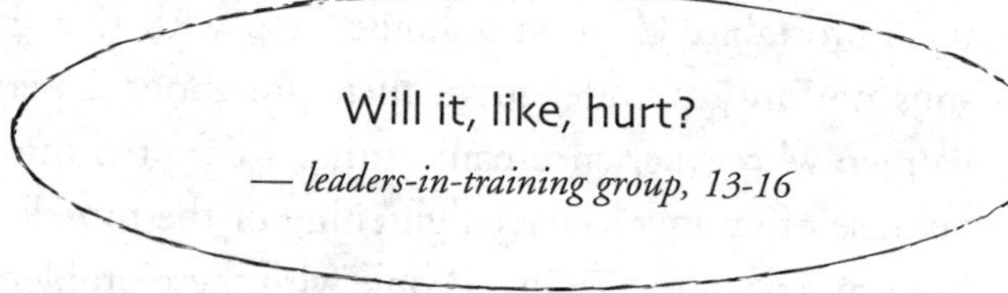

Will it, like, hurt?
— *leaders-in-training group, 13-16*

Maybe, maybe not. For young women having vaginal sex, it depends on a few things:

1. What's up with the young woman's hymen? See the "How To ... " chapter, page 91.

2. Is the female feeling comfortable enough with the situation that the ring of muscle at the opening of her vagina can relax? This includes having a fair degree of trust in the person she's with, liking her own body, wanting to share it, feeling "ready," and not being anxious about interruptions, pregnancy and infection. Whew! Past sexual abuse which has not been dealt with can silently cause the muscles to go into a "Do Not Enter" state.

3. Has her body had enough time to be really warmed up? Her vagina will produce lube quickly; its expansion inward takes more time. (See page 78 for more on that.)

There can be some other less common sources of pain. For guys who are not circumcised, the foreskin may be a bit too snug to draw back easily over the erect head of the penis. Although this situation is generally noticed earlier on, during masturbation, a small number of guys find that during intercourse the extra tension on the foreskin can be uncomfortable. Condoms should help with this. For reasons not always understood, there are about 2 percent of women who experience pain during attempted intercourse because of an involuntary tightening of the muscles in the bottom part of the vagina. People with these problems need to see a medical professional.

For anal sex, the same "ready" feeling applies, except of course the hymen, self-lubrication and expansion are not issues. Going slowly and using lube are key in avoiding discomfort. (See more details on page 86.)

I had sex for the first time last weekend and we didn't use anything. Should I be worried?

— TV call-in, female, 16

If you mean "should I do something about it?", my answer is "yes!" And I don't mean praying for your period! If it's less than three (or even four) days ago, then scoot to a clinic and ask them about the emergency contraceptive pill (Morning-After pill). Then, while you're there, talk about when you can get a first internal exam and what you can use in the future so you don't have to worry! Unless you've decided to swear off ever having sex again (a common oath, that usually lasts a few weeks)!

Why is there always stuff in my underpants?

— girls' health class

Isn't growing up great! Your vaginal fluids become a constant guessing game — *is this normal or not?* When you're turned on, the walls of your vagina make a nice wet lube; this makes intercourse more comfortable. The other healthy stuff that happens to everyone who's not using the Pill or Depo includes some thicker whitish stuff just after and just before your period. A couple of weeks before your period, you may notice a different, clearer, stretchy (like egg white) fluid. That's the sperm-friendly mucus (eewww) your body makes about five days before your egg is released. The egg lives only for a day but the sperm can hang in there for at least five. So, for about a week after this fluid starts up, you are *very fertile.*

Then there's the not-so-friendly stuff that may show up in your undies. For people who've not had intercourse, an unusually curdy, slightly smelly discharge may be a yeast infection. There are some drugstore and home remedies that can clear this up. There are other non-sexually transmitted infections you can get, so have anything that seems weird checked out. If you've gone "all the way," and especially if you've not used a condom, you may have picked up any number of yucky infections. GO GET CHECKED OUT — THIS WEEK!

I'm going on my honeymoon this summer and I've heard that if I keep taking the Pill, I won't get a period; is this safe?

— *online*

Sure, you can juggle around your Pill pack for a special event. If you count ahead and see that the time your period comes lands at a really inconvenient time, you can safely skip over it that month. If your pills all look the same, after taking the first three weeks, pull out a new pack and start them without going through the seven days when your period would usually come. If your pills are triphasic (different colours), check with a clinic or pharmacy about how to do this. Carry on taking the next pack as you usually do. When you're on the Pill, you have sort of a fake period anyway, so not having a flow for a month is no big deal. However, I wouldn't switch around much without first checking in with your medical person.

> I'm not sure if we did it ... I was, like, totally wasted; she seemed to know what she was doing. It was my first time. Should I ask her?
>
> — *counselling session*

The guy who asked me this question did in fact end up asking the person he'd been with. He really wanted to know, because it was his first time. The answer was "yes." He was pissed — at her for being pushy and at himself for letting it happen. He'd made out with lots of girls but hadn't had sex because he'd wanted to wait for the special person. Special this wasn't.

I've been with this guy four times and I still bleed tons; not much when we're having sex, I mean we put a towel down, but after, when I go to the bathroom ... is this normal?

— clinic patient, female, 24

Wow, you're persistent! It's not common to continue to bleed that much after the first few times, but it happens. Sounds like the part of the hymen that's torn needs time to heal — so go back to fooling around without having intercourse for a couple of weeks. If it still bleeds, I'd go get it checked out.

I have CP [cerebral palsy] and can't coordinate my muscles very easily. My [able-bodied] girlfriend and I have talked about having sex. I feel ready to be with her. I'd like to, but I don't know if I can do what I'm supposed to.

— student to a nurse

Good for this guy for finding out what he can ahead of time! The lack of communication about sexual matters from the various professionals to the youth with physical challenges that they deal with is shameful. Of course people with disabilities can have delicious sexual encounters — but it usually takes more preparation than for able-bodied people. Just like in the general population, an individual's pleasure may come ('scuse the pun) as much from other play, like having someone go down on them, as from intercourse. I wish we could move to the place where what we're "supposed" to do is to give and get delightful moments — however we can get that to happen. It's tough to get past the Western culture's pressure to have sex just like they do in all the movies!

> My mom and I talk about lots of stuff, but I don't really feel comfortable telling her how far me and my boyfriend have gone.
>
> — *call-in TV show*

And she, hopefully, doesn't talk about *her* sex life in detail! Being sexually active is something that helps us become separate from our parents. That said, if you have cause for celebration, concerns, or are uncomfortable about what's happening, your mom/dad may be a good person to talk to. When it works, talking about these important things can bring family members closer. You don't have to be real personal; you can start by saying, "I heard that if someone ..."

Is it safer for a girl to have sex before or after her period?

— youth group question

Guys sometimes hear from girls, "Don't worry, it's my safe time." Worry. While there is a "safe time" in a girl's cycle, it takes a lot of training to understand when it is. See the previous question, "Why is there always stuff in my underpants?" or check out the "When are you fertile?" chart on page 114 for more on this.

My boyfriend and I had sex last week. It didn't really hurt, but I didn't have an orgasm, I don't think. Is there something I should be doing?

— grade ten class

According to the (grown-up) women in one survey, a minority actually got physical pleasure the first time, and very few from that group had an orgasm.[23] The ones who enjoyed it the most were a bit older when they first had sex, had figured out how to bring themselves to an orgasm through masturbation, and were experienced at making out up to the point of penetration. By the way, for females especially, orgasms may not always be totally obvious to us. The good news is, with the right lover it only gets better, as long as you can talk about what's working and not working for you!

> If a guy has sex with another guy, does that mean he's gay?
>
> — *high school group*

No. He may be, or he may be "bi" or Two-Spirit (a term used by some aboriginal peoples), or just curious, or something else. It's important for us not to slap a label on ourselves, or on another person, because of who he/she sleeps with. If people choose to label *themselves* straight, gay, bi ... then that's *their* choice.

> My friend says that he can tell if a girl's been done by just looking at her, like, walking down the hall. Is it true?
>
> — *high school*

What, she looks like she's just jumped off a horse?! Pleeease. I've heard lots of variations on this and it is *not* possible to tell if a girl has had sex just by watching her. Really!

For years I've known that my family had arranged my marriage with a boy from our country. The problem is, I've had sex with my boyfriend here. Will the person I'm to marry be able to tell?

— *online*

Hmmm, not an easy situation to be in. No; unless you tell him, your husband will not know you've been with anybody else (nor will you know about him). However, he needs to somehow be informed that not all brides bleed the first time. Maybe you can read parts of this book to him, or visit your doctor together (if he/she's good) to discuss protection, first time, etc. There are times when the bride decides to be honest about her past with the man she's to marry. It can work out well, or be a disaster, depending on the guy's response.

By the way, arranged marriages, particularly where the youth are given some power to accept the match or not (a veto), can work out fine for the couple. It's not as though the modern way of getting together works out that well in many instances; it's just what many of us are used to!! Matching up for marriage is complicated no matter how it's done. There's no "right" way for everyone across every culture.

NOTE: One of the serious problems with expecting females to be "untouched" until the wedding night is trying to prove this. Ignorance and oppression create a notion that first penetration must be difficult. Blood on the sheets is expected, and in some countries where virginity is demanded, the sheets are under public scrutiny. Well, what happens to the poor young thing who was born with hardly any hymen, who was an athlete, or rode horses? It gets worse. What if she were raped — never able to tell anyone? In some cases the groom doesn't care, or he knows better, and will cut himself to provide the blood. Unfortunately, in other cases, where the bride is thought to be "defiled," she is banished or killed. I'm talking the twenty-first century here; this is happening now in some countries around the world.

How can a guy know when a girl's faking it?

— co-ed classroom, 14-19

There is a classic scene in the movie, *When Harry Met Sally,* where Meg Ryan imitates a fake orgasm during lunch, in a restaurant. It's highly believable. As she points out, most women admit to faking an orgasm at some point, and most guys don't know that it's happened — do the math! And it's too bad, because if it's a regular habit, both the female and her partner miss out. Mostly, it starts because the young woman thinks that everybody else is having wild orgasms. She doesn't want to be different and she doesn't want to disappoint her guy. Or she may be bored and want to curl up with her book! Later, if she wants to work on having a real orgasm, it's tough to admit she's been faking it. So goes the circle.

A guy's only way of really knowing is to be aware of the rhythmic muscle contractions that happen in the genitals. There is a wave of three to twelve contractions in these muscles, very much like when a guy comes. But if the contractions aren't strong, or if there aren't many, then it's hard to detect. A better way is to not expect an orgasm only through intercourse, but by touching in other ways. And if you practise being honest with each other, then the fakin' thing is far less likely to happen.

People say sex up the ass can totally damage you, so you have to wear diapers later.

— teen mothers' group

If anal intercourse is done gradually, using lots of lube, with the "bottom" in control, it won't damage the tissue. There have been times when this is not the case, and yes, permanent damage can happen. Also *condoms* are really important to use! (You knew I'd add that.)

My dick bends to the left; will it be a problem when I have sex?

— hot-line caller

Lots of guys have a slight bend; as long as it's not too extreme it shouldn't interfere with intercourse. It may be that you were born like that, or if you got a serious crotch injury, tissue on one side may have been damaged. Making a joke about it before getting naked with somebody may relieve some of the tension you're feeling.

If the bend causes painful erections or seems to make intercourse very difficult, then a doctor needs to be consulted.

What are your chances of catching AIDS using a condom?

— youth group

If you use a condom from start to finish each time? Slim. Couples where one is HIV positive and one is negative often continue to have sex and the uninfected person does not get the virus. Of course your risk level depends on several things. There is an equation[24] used to explain it:

So, as an example, if a couple are not injection-drug users (including injecting steroids), only have oral and vaginal sex and don't have any other illnesses, they'd be at lower risk for HIV even if a condom failed. If you look at another couple who are basically in the same situation, except they also have unprotected anal sex and one of them had lots of previous partners, then that bumps up the exposure risk. Throw into that that she'd had an abnormal Pap test result (probably linked to the STI called HPV), and their risk level is higher still.

The Stooge Table wants to know what's so important about the Pill, and do you have to use a condom with it?

— youth group
(the "Stooge Table" was a group of young guys!)

The Pill is an amazing combination of hormones that basically stops the egg from being released and so prevents pregnancy. (For more detail see the "Protection" chapter.)

Yes, you still have to use condoms. For two reasons. First, the Pill doesn't work all the time, mainly because it's really easy to forget a day or two. Second, it does nothing to stop STIs like chlamydia, which these days you have to assume are sneaking around close by. So put your party hats on, boyz.

When you play around, are girls supposed to shave their pubic hair?

— girls' group, 14–16

Please. I know these days we're being sold on the idea that everything to do with bodies is supposed to be sterile, no natural smell or taste or look. But for young women reading this, please, do what *you want.* Nature has made us this way for a reason and *lots* of the reason has to do with sexual attraction. The hair is there to hold in the pheromones or sex scent, just like underarm hair. Lots of people love the look of a thick "bush" or some scent other than deodorant! If you want to trim, shave, or wax your hair for your own comfort, then fine. But don't assume the person you're with requires it.

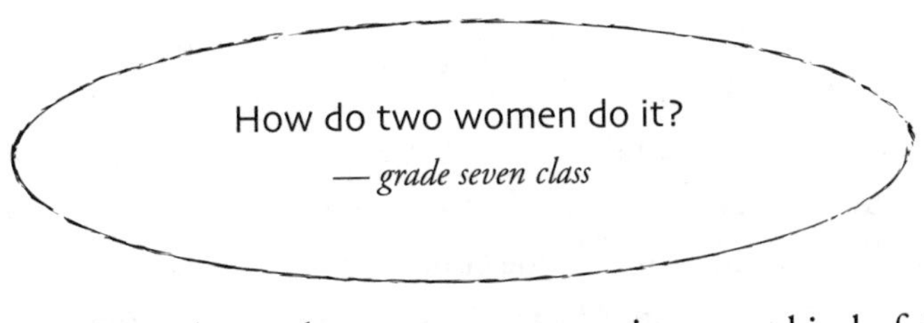

How do two women do it?
— *grade seven class*

Porn always shows two women using some kind of dildo or fake penis in each other, as though that were a necessary part of women having sex. It's not. Humans are able to get and give pleasure with almost every part of their body ... well, maybe not their elbows. No matter whether they're the same or the opposite sex, people can have pleasure by using various body parts — their hands, mouths, nipples — and by rubbing each other's genitals. For fun, same-sex and opposite-sex couples do sometimes use "toys" (like vibrators), but that's totally optional.

What's an orgasm?

— *grade six class*

It's sort of like a sneeze between your knees.[25]
See page 80 in the "How To ... " chapter.

What if you want to go to Grad but you don't want to go all the way?

— *high school girls*

When this question came up, I put it back to the rest of the group. The answers included: "Tell him a couple of days before that you're not ready to sleep with him yet," "Just pretend that you're on [your period]," "Book a room with another couple," "Just say you're not going to," "Say that your mom won't let you stay out all night." It makes me crazy that this is such a pressure that so many teens, including some guys, have to deal with.

I'm not saying that it can't be fun for some couples. One of the older girls in the group talked about how much she and her bf were looking forward to it. They'd been having sex for awhile (responsibly) and were looking forward to a special night, waking up together. Speaking of which — all you parents out there — WAKE UP. If you think that staying at a hotel is just part of an innocent Grad tradition that you have no say in, think again. Make sure your child is comfortable with the plans and be the big bad ogre if you sense ambivalence on her or his part. As for the teens themselves, I agree with the straightforward talk ahead of time — and then don't crawl into bed with the other person at 4:00 am or they'll think you've changed your mind!

How **BIG** is the average penis?

— college journalist, interview

Penis size — such a worry to many guys. Erect, the average full-grown penis is about one and a half inches in diameter and five and a half to six and a half inches in length. Guys often think that other guys are way bigger than this, maybe because of porn — where they only hire guys who are like horses. Females don't help the matter by teasing guys (waving baby fingers). In fact, there are way more complaints on my Web site from guys who are big than small. Remember ...

It's
not the wand;
it's the magician!
(Listen up,
Harry Potter!)

CHAPTER 7

for parents and others (who won't be there)

THOUGHTS FOR ADULTS ...

If you're an adult reading this book, there's a good chance that you're interested in helping a young person work through the difficult decisions they face regarding sex. Your parents/family and teachers did the best job they could helping you, given what was handed to them. You probably want to improve on that. The temptation is to tell youth what "should/shouldn't" happen. As adults we spend lots of time doing this:

You shouldn't tease your brother/sister.
You should be doing eight hours of homework.
You should wait till you're older to have sex.

When we try this tactic with ourselves it doesn't usually work very well ...

I should floss my teeth regularly.
I should get more exercise.
I should be talking about sex stuff with the kids.

What *does* help? We generally get further if we start with the way things really are, rather than how they "should" be. Sticking with "shoulds" is like having your head stuck in the sand — you miss what's actually happening. And even though this approach may feel more comfortable, you will only be of minimal help to a young person if you stick with the "shoulds." There is a difference between giving teens a clear understanding of how you expect them to behave (a good thing), and responding rigidly when things don't go "according to plan."

"The downfall is giving kids too many choices. Kids have a lot of choices, but the best choice is abstinence. I guess they can go elsewhere for more information."[26] Pretending that we can impose our wishes on youth is not only unhelpful to them, it's dangerous. Some youth are conservative by nature and will wait until they're older before having sex; many won't. Sure, families and institutions can discuss what they believe is best for their youth (including why), but by not ensuring that risk-reduction information and material is available, they are shirking their duty and placing young people at risk.

"The big issue for parents is acknowledging that during high school the majority of kids will have had intercourse and that most kids will be having sex by the time they hit twenty."[27] Most adults hope that their children or students will wait until they're older before having sex: age thirty at least! Statistically, for youth who are seventeen years old, about half have had vaginal intercourse. This can vary a lot within the same country — depending on the group of youth. For instance, the age is younger for North American born teens who leave high school early.[28]

While we get worried about youth having sex, for all of the obvious reasons, in doing research for this book I've heard again and again, from people of all ages, that it's not the actual "losing one's virginity" that we should be focusing on. What's more important is how much control young people feel they have over sharing their body and how openly they can communicate about this part of their life. I know from my own experience that it's a challenge to know how to help a young person with this complex area of life, especially when we're met with withering looks. My advice? Carry on!

From: "alex*"<crazy_4u1@idmail.com>
To: bebe@idmail.com
Subject: ewww!
Date: Thu, Dec 2002 20:23:58 -0500

Hi Bebe! What's up?!

Omg, my mom just tried to talk to me about sex for the first time! How old am i again? I think it's a little late for her to be telling me what a condom is. It pisses me off so bad, cause she thinks i know nothing about anything. It's just like that stupid sex teacher who told us what our periods were like two years after most of us had gotten them. I was thinking of telling her that i have had sex already, but i know she'll freak out or try and talk to me even more (which is what i don't want.) Anyways it's my business, not hers. She'll ask about the guy, what protection we used and all that shit. I can't even bring the subject up without her acting all weird. You're so lucky you have parents that understand stuff. mail me back soon, k?

xo-alex-xo

With the "screenagers" in our lives today, it's hard to figure out what they know and where the information gaps are. Generally, it's safe to assume that they've been exposed to much more than we think they have!

What gets in the way for some adults is the worry that if we say anything informative or anything that acknowledges the likelihood that sex is around the corner, we are "encouraging" it. But as one mother of four told me, "the pretend-it-doesn't-exist approach we grew up with sucked."

We give young people tons of information about drugs and smoking without worrying that they're going to rush out and try them the first chance they get. We need to think about information related to sexual matters in the same way.

I assume that you're not expecting me to come up with a recipe for how to approach the subject of sex ... but that's what I've done! It's an example of trying to "lighten up" when we approach this topic with youth, since that's one of the complaints they have! Some of you may say, "but it's a very serious subject ... " True enough. However, as many of you already know, youth aren't very receptive to the heavy-handed approach. Good communication, starting with the important adults in their lives, is not the only thing youth need in order to make good choices, but it is one of the key components.

This Season's Recipe for a Fresh and Healthy Sex Talk with Kids

***Preparation time including cooking** — years, in 30 minute sessions*

***Makes** — one youth with a greater chance at sexual health*

- 2 points of view
- 2 willing people
- 1 quiet place
- dash of humour
- 2 beverages or snacks (if sitting)
- good ongoing communication
- handful of good questions
- pinch of advice

This recipe works best if used before age ten, but cooking it up anytime is better than never. Fortunately for me, it was my father's favourite approach when I was growing up. He tried to make sexuality just a normal thing.

Walking or a drive in the car (with cell phones off) allows for the uninterrupted mixing of views. Sharing concerns and clarifying what's going on in the youth's personal life needs to unfold respectfully, with a large measure of affirmation added — "I think you handled blah-blah-blah well, and I'm wondering about this weekend ... " This can help to offset the curdling or separation that frequently happens between adults and youth.

When differing points of view bubble up, breathe deeply and listen. Listen some more.

Fold in an acknowledgement such as, "It's not always easy to talk about this stuff ... "

This particular concoction is never really finished, but you'll have some fine morsels to share if you become familiar with the recipe. Remember to keep the heat on low and stir with great care. Expect nothing over thirty minutes max.

Recipe for Lite Sexuality Chat with Children

***Preparation time** —*
best to do some planning for discussion, which is often 15–30 minutes
***Makes** — one better prepared youth*

- 1 willing person (youth or adult)
- 1 reluctant person
- 1 semi-quiet place
- dash of humour
- bunch of other resources

This time-cheater recipe can work in the less-than-perfect situation most adults find themselves in these days. It strongly appeals to fast-food fans. One person has a point to make or a request. The other person is not "available" due to any number of factors including: an aversion to this kind of discussion, a favourite TV show, not seeing the subject as important and so on.

The person who is motivated to talk needs to make sure the other person is as undistracted as possible (not in front of the TV, heading out the door, studying/working, dyeing their hair ...).

There needs to be some agreement that a short, calm discussion can happen. This brew will bubble over and burn very quickly. So when it seems that's about to happen, turn off the heat; maybe even leave the kitchen for a minute!

Either person can dish out written material that supports their viewpoint (stats on teen STI rates, clinic locations, articles on parenting ...).

A small, simple action plan can also be successfully thrown in at the end. For example, "So then, I'd appreciate it if you leave your bedroom door open when you're in there together." Best to remain focused on a single dish. (Don't throw in the kitchen sink.)

My job as a parent is to be sure you know this stuff ... I could lose my Parent License if we don't talk!

Recipe for Disaster

Preparation time — zip
Makes — one youth at higher risk
(They'll be toast.)

- 2 or more people unwilling to discuss sexual matters
- no time set aside
- high level of advice-giving
- low level of listening
- bushel of mistrust

This particular creation is one we've all tasted at one time or another and is often described as tasting sour or bitter. It leaves both people feeling empty and angry. This is a most dangerous situation for young people, who need lots of nurturing.

While there may be little verbal communication, there are still plenty of "messages" being dished out. There is no such thing as no message when it comes to sex. Anti-sex, anti-gay, anti-youth messages can be smelled, like something rotten in the fridge.

Just as with the other recipes, families tend to pass this

way of interacting down from one generation to the next, unless someone makes an effort at improving their skills and ability to be accepting of others. When this effort does happen, generally with input from a professional, more savoury interactions can happen quickly. If adults can get out to cooking classes, they can get to parent classes too! (Though I know of none that are offered together ...)

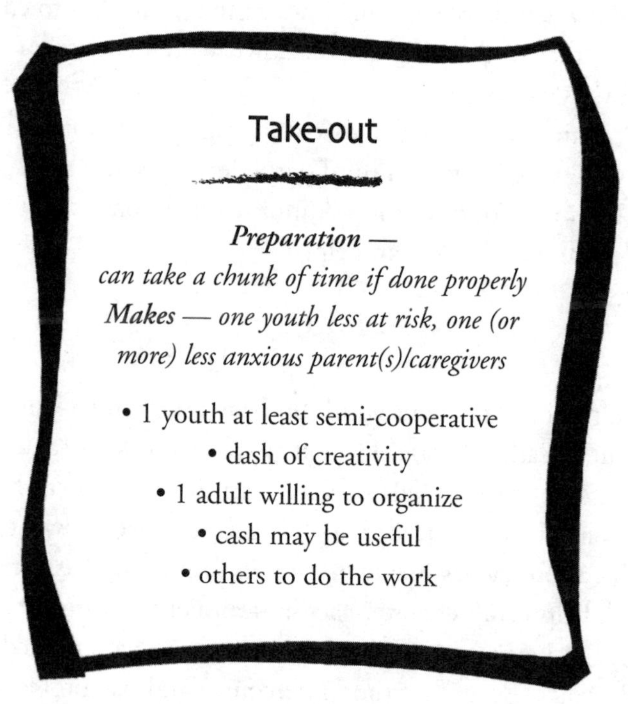

Take-out

Preparation *—*
can take a chunk of time if done properly
Makes *— one youth less at risk, one (or more) less anxious parent(s)/caregivers*

- 1 youth at least semi-cooperative
- dash of creativity
- 1 adult willing to organize
- cash may be useful
- others to do the work

This is a fabulous alternative available to adults when that feeling of "oh no, not me, I'm not going to talk about this" presents itself. While not everybody can talk about sexual matters, it's still the *adult's job* to make sure that it happens, just like it's the adult's job to provide proper nutrition.

Parents can ask for help from somebody their son or daughter is connected with — a sibling, relative, teacher or youth leader ... Teachers can invite in a colleague or guest who is more comfortable with the topic. Teens and parents/guardians will sometimes go to a sexual health clinic together so that they can sit down with a counsellor … really, I've seen this!

Again, solutions for specific disagreements are often helped along by using a third party; let's hope not as a substitute for talking, but in addition to it. Books, hot-lines, videos and Web sites can help.

Adults who care about youth do have much to be worried about. Death. Disease. Pregnancy. Heartbreak. Assault. In an attempt to keep kids safe, we often try to frighten them or control them. Studies on this subject have shown that while those tactics may work on an immediate basis, they don't help youth choose to act in healthier ways afterwards. Over and over, research has indicated that what's needed to help youth delay first-time intercourse and use protection when they do have sex is:

- a sense of hope for their future (school, sports, work, relationships ...)
- accurate and *useful* information, including birth

control info and stuff about pleasure

- a chance to discuss common real-life situations and possible responses
- access to clinical services and counselling that are geared to youth
- a strong relationship with a close adult who can discuss real situations, feelings ...

It's no wonder that youth, especially in the United States but also in Canada and the UK, are still at such risk. While funding has been given to sex-ed programs, when they are abstinence-only focused and do not take into account the above needs, they are bound to fail.

And thus we fail our youth. It is not enough that an adult gives a young person the information and confidence they need. We must fight for the resources and support that all youth need. This includes the basics of living — food, shelter, safety. A look at international statistics shows that it is possible to have more sexually healthy youth without having to lock 'em all up!

When I speak with parents' groups, many people come to the session with specific concerns. Let's have a look at some of these.

Having Sex Too Young

Lots of parents worry that their son, but especially their

daughter, will end up having sex when they are too young (the kid, not them). "The parent's main role in the question of sex is education, but most of that should already have taken place by the time their children become teens. Teenagers want to hear lots about sex, but not from their parents."[29] Providing books (like this one!) and access to other sources of information is one important thing parents can do. The time for parents to do the education is *before* children hit their teens. Once children have crossed over into those years, you can share your concerns and values, but they are not going to happily chat about making out or protection.

You could try something like this:

> *I know you're probably pretty clear about where I stand on the sex issue … that I'd like you to wait till you're [older, married, finished school …]. However, what's most important is that you stay safe and healthy, and so if you choose to have sex earlier, please do talk to someone who knows lots about protection — like the youth clinic counsellor. I'm guessing you know all about how important it is to use condoms right from the start … And in case I've never said this out loud, I think that two people being together is very special, and I hope it will be a positive thing for you …*

Can you actually control your child's behaviour? Not let them date? Tell them they're forbidden from having sex until marriage? Not let them have friends over when you're

out? Dream on!

From working in youth clinics for years, I have heard in detail the kinds of lies and schemes teens use to get around their household's rules. One young woman whose parents were extremely strict with her, including drop-off and pick-up from a girls' high school, got pregnant when she and her boyfriend had sex in his car at lunch time. How she had her abortion is another story ...

Providing adequate supervision and additional information can help, but "in today's world teenagers do have the freedom and the opportunity to have sex if they really want to ... Parents delude themselves if they believe otherwise."[30] At this point, your main job is to be as supportive as possible, set reasonable (?!) expectations, and hope that the values and life skills you've passed on to your daughter/son will serve them well.

> I personally don't think that, in today's culture, rigid rules work very well. I've found that negotiating guidelines for the teen's activities, which include consequences when the agreements are broken, is most effective. The bottom line is our kid's safety, and if we put them in the position where they have to lie to us and sneak around, they will be at greater risk.

SLEEPOVERS

In some households, a girl or guy will approach their parent/guardian about allowing their boyfriend or girlfriend to sleep over, in their room. There are adults who will agree, others will say "no way." What's it depend on?

In part, your values, their age, their level of maturity, how long they've been together. There may be special circumstances such as difficult transportation home. You'll factor in other siblings in the household and where their rooms are! And while it may not be entirely fair — there's the point of whether or not you like the bf/gf.

Of course this request will come at 10:00 at night, not the best time to discuss it, so don't, right then. I don't think there is a right or wrong answer here. Several factors need to be considered. As my friend clearly heard from her sixteen year old daughter, "don't assume because we're alone in a bed we're having sex." There may only be cuddling happening, really.

On the flip side, if they really want to start having sex, a couple can find a way to sneak it in; they don't need a sleepover. However, in the final analysis, it's your home and young people need to respect that.

BF, mother of a sixteen year old daughter, said, "I know my daughter would be responsible, and I like her boyfriend, and if he stays with her overnight I'm not going to make any assumptions about what they're up to. I'd rather them be together here than somewhere not at all private or safe."

DM, father of a seventeen year old daughter, said, "I know it sounds old-fashioned, but I'm not OK with her boyfriend staying over ... what would we say to our ten-year-old?"

> Another thing that parents sometimes run into that didn't happen "when we were growing up" is mixed (guys and girls) sleepovers. Not an orgy, just hanging out together and then sleeping all in the same room.

In most cases, if the young person is living at home, the parent(s) would rather not have to deal with it. Same with coming home for a weekend from college/university. This goes for daughters especially. Some corner of our brain may think the young person is "going at it" but lots of adults take the "I'd-rather-not-know" position! Once they're married or over age forty (or both) this may change! Until then, we'd rather kids just sneak around if they're going to do it! Funny messages, eh?!

Sharing Past Experiences

"Did you and dad do it before you were married?" ... Just the kind of question to send a parent running. Adults wonder how much about their own experiences as youth they need to or should share — drug use, sex, the time they got kicked out of school, and so forth.

I think there are times when we can share a past experience and have two positive things happen. First, it may lead to greater openness within the relationship, and this is a good thing. Second, through sharing our story, a young person may see their situation in a slightly different light. Of course they may also toss it back at us saying, "Well, you had sex before you were married ... " Here are some guidelines that may help:

- Tell a story; don't lecture.
- Tell your own story, not others', or exclude names if it's someone the kid knows.
- Especially with sexual matters — there is no need to

go into great detail!

- You can suggest that they keep the information confidential, but don't share anything that you don't want your kid's friends' parents' friends to know!
- If you're asked a question that feels too personal, you can always say, "that's kind of personal for me."

Supplying Condoms

Parents who are willing to admit that their son or daughter is likely to be having sex in the near future (if they aren't already) wonder if they should have a supply of condoms around. Not necessarily by the front door, but perhaps in the bathroom drawer. They worry that they may be giving the "wrong message," the "Just-Do-It" message. They're concerned about what other adults will think.

My opinion — good for you for keeping 'doms around the house! As though a kid is going to run right out and have sex 'cause there's a box of condoms around! I warn you, though; they may be used for water balloons at times! Because a household or agency that has condoms around is also more likely to approach the topic of sexuality more openly, the teen will feel more prepared to deal with the outside pressure. Also, condoms aren't cheap, and, like bus tickets, they're never right there when you need one!

Not Liking or Trusting the Boyfriend/ Girlfriend

What can you do?! Not much. If you decide to say anything, which you may not, since it could have the opposite of the intended effect, choose your timing and words wisely. I'd say give it your best shot and then zip up your lip after that. Let's hope that statistics will prevail and the relationship won't last!

A more serious situation is when you have evidence that your kid is with someone who is abusive towards them. When you raise your concern (which of course you should), stick with concrete examples: what you saw, heard or were told. Anyone in this situation is at first full of denial and excuses. What you want to avoid is driving your child closer to this person, isolating them from you. Getting advice from someone knowledgeable in this area can help.

Sexual assault/coercion

It's amazing the number of young women I've seen at clinics who were forced or coerced into having sex and would not even consider telling the adults closest to them. They are embarrassed and afraid of being blamed. This goes for guys too. Generally the girls were sexually assaulted or raped by a guy that they knew, often the person they were going out with. If your child or client tells you or hints to you that they have experienced some kind of forced sexual activity, here is the list to follow:

1. Tell them it *was not* their fault — even if they've gone against your rules.
2. Acknowledge that they were brave to talk about it; that it's important.
3. Ask if they'd be willing to talk to a doctor/nurse (if

penetration occurred), or hot-line counsellor.

DO NOT:

1. Freak out (even if you're supportive, they'll regret telling you).
2. Force them to do anything unwillingly. (They've already been forced.)
3. Ask any question that implies that it was their fault. ("Why did you go ... ")

For more detail on this issue, check out the "Not Your Choice" chapter.

THOUGHTS FOR TEENS — WHEN ADULTS ARE THE ISSUE

Part of becoming sexually active with someone is that your family (or those closest to you) will have some opinion about the matter — if they know about it. Even if you live on the other side of the world from them, they'll have some questions! Even if you try hard to cover up the fact that you are, or were, with someone, you can hear their questions in your head! You can't get around it! Unless you are very young, this is a private part of your life and you do not actually *have* to share anything with others. But if you can trust the older person (or sib), then letting them in on this part of your life can be a bonus.

DATING

As you know, there are some families that don't allow their

kids, especially their daughters, to date before a certain time. When you live in a Western culture, where dating is seen as "normal," this can be hard.

Young people I've spoken with handle this in several ways. Some comply with their family's rules — they may hang out with guys and girls in a group, but not one-to-one. Some mainly go along with it, but secretly have a bf/gf who they talk with on the phone, chat online and spend time with in a group and at school; but they don't really go out on "dates." And then there are youth who pretty much ignore their family rules and either lie like crazy or openly go against them.

What's fair? Well, when you live under your family's roof, they have the right to make the rules. You can see if there is any openness to shifting some of the rules. Choose a good time and place to talk ... like not right when they get in from work.

And if you don't want to go the route of lying and sneaking around, then you have to show your parents you are trustworthy. If you do decide to go behind their backs, remember that lies are *often* found out and then things are worse than before! Adults can soften on decisions — but it takes time.

Finally, while it may not feel like it, you won't be under their roof forever!

Sleepovers

If you've been together for awhile (and I don't mean just a

couple of weeks) and hung around each other's family, you may wonder if it's OK to talk to mom/dad about your sweetie sleeping over, in your bed.

If you don't want to keep quiet about your desire to have your bf/gf "sleep" with you, I suggest having a general talk about it with parents, maybe based on something from a TV program or someone else's situation. This can help parents think about different points of view without all the intensity of their own specific situation.

Of course within the same household, two parents may not hold the same view. "Not unless you're married," one may say. And while some parents concede that there are times when they'd consider allowing their kids to have their "friend" sleep over, they may point out that there are others who also have to be considered — like siblings and the other family.

Check out the section for parents (above) to get an idea of the things parents have to think about. And unless you know that your family would be cool with this, don't spring the question or ask it with others around.

My opinion about having your bf/gf stay over? Nice if it can happen, especially if your room is not right beside your folks' or siblings', but while you're under your parents' roof, you need to respect their decision about getting under the sheets. You won't be living there forever!

Embarrassment

You may think that we, as parents or teachers, are going out of our way to try to embarrass you with the way we give you sex-ed info, but we're usually just trying to do what we can to protect you! So please be patient with the books and looks and talks!

If the adults in your life keep mute on this subject, it's often because they're too shy to bring it up or don't know how. They may also think you're too young to know anything about sex. (Little do they know.) So *you* raise the subject. ("Yeah, right!" most of my students say.) You can use something that came up in class, on TV or with other people to break the ice. For those who have a parent/guardian who you know won't discuss the "S" word, there may be a friend's parent, a teacher or another adult who is happy to yak about this.

CHAPTER 8

still wondering ... more info

In *All The Way* I've tried to cover some of the common situations young people may find themselves in. But since we're all unique, there are probably other specific questions you have. Here's a list of free hot-lines, some videos, Web sites and books that I hope will be helpful now and in the future! Some of these are also for parents, teachers and other adults.

HOT-LINES

(all confidential)

Facts of Life Line (Planned Parenthood)

1-800-463-6739

This is an automated tape series covering a whole range of sexual topics.

Kids Help Phone

1-800-668-6868 (anywhere in Canada)

The staff at this hot-line can help you deal with a wide

range of issues, including sexual abuse/assault, questions about being straight, gay, bi ... and "am-I-normal" stuff. They can also give you information about other numbers to call or places you could go.

Lesbian and Gay, Bi Youth Line

1-800-268-9688

Peer counsellors — hours are Sunday to Friday 4:00 – 9:30 pm.

Parents' Help Line

1-888-603-9100 (anywhere in Canada)

Professionals are available to discuss child- and youth-related concerns with parents/caregivers.

Sexual Health and AIDS Hot-lines

1-800-661-4337 British Columbia
1-800-772-2437 Alberta
1-800-667-6876 Saskatchewan
1-800-782-2437 Manitoba
1-800-668-2437 Ontario
1-800-263-1638 Quebec
1-800-561-4009 New Brunswick
1-800-314-2437 PEI
1-800-566-2437 Nova Scotia
1-800-563-1575 Newfoundland and Labrador
1-800-661-0507 Yukon
1-800-661-0795 Nunavut

Counsellors give info on a variety of sexuality topics, including STIs and AIDS.

Large number of languages spoken — call to find out.

STD/STI/AIDS Hot-lines in the USA

1-800-342-2437 or 1-800-227-8922
(Spanish 1-800-344-7432)

Web sites

www.casac.ca

The Canadian Association of Sexual Assault Centres looks at the legal and social changes needed to prevent and eventually stop sexual assault. Under "Anti-Violence Centres," there is a list of rape crisis centres and shelters across Canada.

www.durexhealthcare.com

Sponsored by Durex condoms, this site has excellent international and British links.

www.goaskalice.columbia.edu/

Go Ask Alice was one of the first good Q&A sites and it's still going strong. Good section for guys as well as girls.

www.hc-sc.gc.ca/pphb-dgspsp/

This clumsy looking address belongs to Health Canada's Centre for Disease Control and it has everything you'd ever want to know about STI/STDs — except pictures! Go to "S" (for STD) under the "A-Z index."

www.Not-2-Late.com

This emergency contraception Web site operates out of Princeton University in the USA. It gives information about various methods, as well as where to obtain the pills in your community. In Canada go to the local or national Planned Parenthood site or number.

www.pflag.org

Parents and Friends of Lesbian and Gay youth (PFLAG) 416-406-1727

An information and support service, especially helpful for parents with kids who have just "come out."

www.teenwire.com

Teenwire (Planned Parenthood Federation of America). For teens and adults, good links.

www.sexualhealth.com

Offers information and further resources on a huge range of subjects. Has a good section on sexuality and people with disabilities, illness and other health-related challenges.

www.sxetc.org

"For teens by teens" (not entirely). Rutgers University, USA.

Offers an inclusive, broad range of info. No positive first-time stories, unfortunately.

Books

Bell, Alexander Ruth. *Changing Bodies, Changing Lives: A Book for Teens on Sex and Relationships,* third edition. New York: Times Books, 1998.

For a book written by an adult, many teens find this author's non-judgmental approach helpful.

Bourgeois, Paulette and Wolfish, Martin. *Changes in You and Me — a book about puberty mostly for girls/boys,* Toronto: Somerville House Publishing, 1994.

Good books on puberty; Kim Martyn served as consultant.

Johanson, Sue. *Talk Sex: Answers to Questions You Can't Ask Your Parents.* Toronto: Penguin Canada, 1988.

A classic from the well known "Sex Lady," this book is based on Q&As from Sue's TV show. Still entertaining and informative for both parents and youth.

Pavanel, Jane. *The Sex Book.* Montreal: Lobster Press, 2001.

Offers A to Z information about sex for youth.

St. Stephen's Community House. *The Little Black Book: A Book on Healthy Sexuality Written By Grrrls For Grrrls.* Toronto, 2000. (416 537-8334)

Since this book was written by young women (who have their facts right), it sits easily with youth. It is by and about young women, but guys and adults often find it informative as well.

Wolf, Anthony, E. *Get Out of My Life — But First Could You Drive Me and Cheryl to the Mall?* New York: The Noonday Press, 1991.

A parent's guide to the new teenager. This is a good parenting book, with a section on sexuality. (Heterosexual focus.)

Videos

Out: Stories of Gay and Lesbian Youth. National Film Board 1993.

This documentary is directed towards youth, but adults will find it informative. Inexpensive, can be accessed through www.nfb.ca.

You Oughta Know: abuse in dating. Kineticvideo.com. 1997. 23 minutes, Canadian (416 538-6613, in the USA call 716 856-7631).

This is a very good educational video for teens focusing on power and all forms of abuse in dating relationships. Urban setting. Not scripted. (Heterosexual depiction only.)

GLOSSARY

Abortion: When a pregnancy is ended using a medical procedure or medication.

Abstinence: Means not doing something; for teens it generally refers to not having sexual intercourse.

AIDS (**acquired immune deficiency syndrome**): A disease caused by a virus (HIV, the human immunodeficiency virus) that destroys the body's immune system. Spread mainly through blood and sexual fluids.

Anal sex: When a penis or other object is inserted into the anus or "butt hole." Also called "freaky" sex.

Anus: Known as the "butt hole" or "poop shoot," this is the opening that leads from the digestive tract.

Arousal: Feeling sexually excited or horny.

Bacteria: Single-celled organisms that can cause disease.

Bi: Slang for bisexual, a person who is attracted to both males and females.

Birth control pill: Often just called "the Pill," this is a series of hormone pills which a female may take to avoid getting pregnant. Does not protect against STIs.

Birth control: Various methods or devices used to prevent pregnancy.

Blow job: Slang for oral sex performed on a guy. ("Blowing" not actually involved!)

Busting: Slang for ejaculation.

Cervix: The lower part of the uterus that opens into the vagina.

Chlamydia: A sexually transmitted infection (STI) caused by bacteria. If left untreated it may cause pelvic inflammatory disease (PID) and infertility. Guys get it too.

Circumcision: The removal of the foreskin from the head of penis.

Clitoris: An amazingly sensitive sex organ in females; looks like a small penis tucked up under a "hood" between the opening of the urethra and the pubic bone. There are two larger parts inside that run either side of the vagina back towards the anus.

Coercion: To pressure or force someone into doing something.

Conception: The result of fertilization, when the egg implants in the uterus.

Condom: Used to prevent pregnancy and the spread of sexually transmitted infections. For males, a thin stretchy tube, usually made of latex, that covers the penis during sex. For females, a polyurethane pouch that is inserted into the vagina before sex (seeing is believing).

Consent: When a person agrees to and gives permission for something. Legally, all sexual activity must have both people's consent.

Contraception: Anything used to stop conception.

Cum: Slang for male ejaculate or semen. Also used as a verb; to ejaculate and/or come to orgasm (male or female). Proper spelling is "come."

Date rape: Intercourse or penetration that's forced on one person by the person they're going out with or dating. A form of sexual assault, and therefore a crime.

Depo-Provera: A hormone method of birth control which is given as a needle every three months. Mainly acts by stopping ovulation. Also called "the Shot."

Diaphragm: A cap-shaped rubber contraceptive used along with spermicide. Fits over the female's cervix during intercourse. It's then washed and can be reused.

Dildo: Made in the shape of a penis of various materials; used as a sex toy or for condom demos.

Discharge: Fluid coming from a body opening; can be normal or the sign of a problem.

Dyke: Slang for lesbian.

Ectopic pregnancy: A pregnancy in which the fertilized egg has implanted somewhere other than in the uterus. Often the location is one of the Fallopian tubes.

Egg: The common term used for the ovum or the female sex cell which grows in the ovary.

Ejaculation: When semen comes out of the penis, usually during an orgasm. Some females have a different kind of fluid that can come out of the urethra. (See G-spot.)

Erection: When the penis (or clitoris) becomes enlarged and harder because of an extra flow of blood into the tissue.

Estrogen: One of two female sex hormones (the other is progesterone) produced in large quantities by the ovaries after puberty and before menopause. Males also make small amounts.

Fallopian tubes: Very narrow tubes connecting the ovaries with the uterus.

Female genital mutilation (FGM): Also called female circumcision. This is a cultural ritual performed on female children which involves altering the genitals. Can range from a small cut to complete elimination of the external genitals, including the clitoris. The more extreme version often seriously affects the woman's health and sexual enjoyment. Now illegal in many countries.

Fertilization: When the egg (or ovum) and the sperm join; part of conception.

Fetus: The term used for an unborn infant after the eighth week of pregnancy.

Fooling around: Slang for sexual touching that doesn't include intercourse.

Foreskin: The loose skin covering the end or head of the penis that boys are born with.

French kissing: Kissing with an open mouth using your tongue.

Gay: A common word for male homosexual; can also include women.

Genitals: The male and female sex and reproductive organs, especially those on the outside.

Going down: A common term for any kind of oral sex on a male or female.

Gonorrhea: A common sexually transmitted infection (STI) caused by bacteria.

G-spot: Called the Grafenberg spot. A small sensitive area found on the front wall of the vagina; for some females can result in female ejaculation. During self-pleasuring or with a partner, some females will have an intense orgasm and release a noticeable amount of clear fluid that is not urine through the urethra.

Hepatitis: Types A, B or C; a virus that infects the liver. Can be sexually transmitted, especially B.

Herpes: Painful blisters caused by a virus usually found on the lips (cold sores) and genitals. If the outbreak is on or inside the genitals, it can easily be spread though sex.

Heterosexual: A person who is (mainly) sexually and emotionally attracted to people of the opposite gender.

HIV: Human immunodeficiency virus; the virus that eventually results in AIDS.

Ho: Slang, short for whore, meaning a female who is very sexual or sleeps with lots of guys. Used as a put-down.

Homophobia: The strong, irrational fear of people who are homosexual.

Homosexual: A person who is (mainly) sexually and emotionally attracted to people of the same gender.

Hooking up: A casual sexual encounter (can also mean just getting together with friends).

Hormone: A chemical messenger that travels through the bloodstream to other glands and organs affecting their activity. Affects sexual maturation, functioning and feeling.

Horny: Slang for sexually excited.

HPV: Human papilloma virus; an STI that causes abnormal growth of cells on and inside the genitals. There are over seventy types; some can cause genital warts, and others may lead to cancer of the cervix if left untreated.

Hymen: The thin membrane of tissue around the opening of the vagina that many girls are born with. If it's still in place at first sexual intercourse, may cause bleeding.

Immune system: The mechanisms in the body that are used to fight off bacteria, viruses and cancerous cells. Includes our own bacteria and antibodies.

Infertility: A man or woman not being able to make a baby.

IUD: The Intrauterine Device is placed into a woman's uterus in order to prevent pregnancy. Made of plastic and sometimes a hormone, it stays in the uterus for a long period of time.

Jerking off: Slang for male masturbation. Also, when someone else uses their hand to make a guy come.

Labia: The two sets of "lips" or folds of skin around the openings of the vagina and the urethra.

Lesbian: A common word for a female who's attracted to other women.

LGBTTQI: Lesbian, gay, bi, transgender, Two-Spirit, queer, intersexed. A catchall for everybody not "straight."

Lovebite: Also know as a "love bruise" or "hickey."

Making out: Slang for sexual touching that doesn't include intercourse.

Masturbation: When a person rubs or touches their own genitals and other sensitive parts of the body in order to have sexual pleasure, usually including an orgasm; self-pleasuring.

Menstruation: A part of a female's cycle (when she's not pregnant) in which the lining of special blood and tissue in the uterus is released through the vagina. Often happens about once every four weeks.

Messing around: Same as making out.

Morning-After pill: Also called emergency contraception, these hormone pills are taken to help prevent a pregnancy. Must be used within three days of unprotected sex.

Mucus: A fluid made by the moist membranes in the body such as the cervix.

Nipple: The sensitive, raised dark area on the breast of males and females. In women, it contains the outlets for milk ducts.

Nonoxynol-9: "N-9"; a chemical used in most "spermicide" products (products which kill sperm). Produced as foam, gel and film; can cause irritation for some females or males.

Oral sex: When one person stimulates another person's genitals with their mouth. Other terms: blow job, going down, muff diving, giving head.

Orgasm: An intense experience that happens at the height of sexual excitement. Caused by increase blood flow and muscle tension, it results in a series of rhythmic contractions felt in the genitals and beyond. Often called "coming" ("cumming").

Ovaries: Two small organs located on each side of the female's uterus that produce the ova (eggs) and female sex hormones.

Ovulation: The release of an ovum (egg) from the ovary.

Pap test: Part of the "internal" exam for females; an important way to check for abnormal cells on the cervix. Generally done yearly after first-time intercourse.

Pelvic exam: Also called the "internal" or Pap, this medical exam makes sure the genitals and reproductive organs of a female are healthy and free from STIs.

Penis: The male sex organ that releases both urine and semen (but not at the same time!).

Period: See Menstruation. *Not* the dot at the end of the sentence!

PID: Pelvic inflammatory disease is usually the result of an untreated STI that spreads up into the uterus and tubes. Dangerous; can lead to sterility (no pregnancy) or ectopic pregnancy.

Pornography: Written or visual material that is intended to cause sexual arousal, rather than education. Considered "adult" entertainment.

Premature ejaculation: A fancy term for when a guy comes more quickly than he wants to.

Progesterone: One of two female sex hormones (the other is estrogen) produced in large quantities by the ovaries after puberty and before menopause. Males also make small amounts.

Prostate gland: A gland in males that surrounds the urethra, below the bladder. Releases fluid into the semen on its way out of the body. Part of male's sexual arousal system.

Puberty: The time when a child develops physically and emotionally into a young adult. Afterwards, most are able to reproduce; generally starts around age ten to twelve.

Pubic hair: Body hair that grows around the genitals.

Queer: Slang for LGBTTQI.

Rape: Forced sexual intercourse: oral, anal or vaginal. See Sexual assault.

Safer sex: Steps that people take to reduce their risk of a pregnancy and/or STI (sexually transmitted infection). Often includes condom use or avoiding unprotected intercourse.

Self-pleasuring: A more positive word for masturbation.

Semen: A whitish mixture of sperm and fluid that's released from the male's urethra during ejaculation (coming).

Sexual assault: Any unwanted sexual touching of a male or female, including all forms of intercourse (rape).

Sexual intercourse: When the penis enters the vagina or anus.

Sexual orientation: Who a person is attracted to both sexually and emotionally; the person may identify as LGBTTQI (lesbian, gay, bi, transgender, Two-Spirit, queer, intersexed) straight or whatever suits them.

Sexuality: A part of who we are from birth till death that includes our gender, orientation, attitudes, feelings and behaviours towards others and ourselves. May not include having "sex."

Sexually transmitted infections/diseases: STIs or STDs are infections we can catch during different kinds of sexual activity from others who have them. Some of the common kinds are HPV, herpes, HIV, chlamydia and gonorrhea.

69: Two people giving/getting oral sex at the same time.

Sperm: The sex cell produced in a male's testicles (balls) after he reaches puberty.

Spermicide: See Nonoxynol-9.

Stereotype: An oversimplified and generalized way of understanding people who belong to a certain group (women/man, black/white, youth/elderly).

Sterile: Not able to produce children.

Straight: A person who is "heterosexual" or attracted to people of the opposite sex.

Syphilis: A sexually transmitted infection that can be cured. One common early sign is a painless blister that appears for a while in the genital/anal area. Dangerous if not treated.

Testicles: The two male sex organs which produce sperm. They hang outside the body in the "scrotum" or sacs of skin. Also called "balls."

Testosterone: A male sex hormone, mainly made in the testicles. Also found at lower levels in females.

Transgender: Abbreviated "trans"; people who cross the boundaries of the sex and/or gender they were given at birth.

Two-Spirit: A term now used by some North American aboriginal peoples who identify themselves as LGBTTQI.

Urethra: The tube in both genders that urine (pee) passes through; in males also the passageway for semen leaving the body.

Uterus: Also called "womb," this organ in females is where a fetus grows.

Vagina: A soft, stretchy tube of muscle that connects a female's uterus with the outside world! The place the penis enters during intercourse.

Vaginitis: Refers to any inflammation of the vagina. Three extremely common types are trichomoniasis, bacterial vaginosis and yeast infections. Can cause an odd, smelly discharge and/or pain when peeing. Easily cured. Can be passed along during intercourse.

Virgin: A male or female who has not gone "all the way"; i.e. hasn't had sex.

Virus: A kind of germ that causes infection. Generally you can treat but not cure viral STIs.

Vulva: The external genitals of a female … what she can see using a hand mirror.

Withdrawal: Also called pulling out; a method of birth control used by guys which involves pulling the penis out of the vagina just before he ejaculates. See the "Protecting Yourself" chapter for more on this.

Yeast infection: Officially called candidiasis, this is an overgrowth of healthy organisms in the vagina which can cause a weird discharge and odour. See Vaginitis.

NOTES

1. Eleanor Maticka-Tyndale, "Sexual Health and Canadian Youth: How do we measure up?" *The Canadian Journal of Human Sexuality* 10, no. 1-2 (2001), 1.

2. Rosalind Miles, *The Women's History of the World* (New York Harper Row, 1988).

3. Bruce M. King, *Human Sexuality Today* (New Jersey: Prentice Hall, 1996), 9.

4. From the video, *You Oughta Know: abuse in dating* (Kineticvideo.com. 1997).

5. S.N. Seidman and R.O. Rieder, "A Review of Sexual Behavior in the USA," *The American Journal of Psychiatry*, March 1994.

6. Melissa Daly, "Sex Smarts," *Seventeen Magazine,* January 2003, 118.

7. Kendall-Tackett, Williams and Finkelhor, "Impact of Sexual Abuse on Children: A Review and Synthesis of Recent Empirical Studies," *Psychological Bulletin 113* (1993), 164-180.

8. Curtis McMillen, Susan Zuravin and Gregory Rideout, "Perceived Benefit from Child Sexual Abuse," *Journal of Consulting and Clinical Psychology* 63 (1995), 1037-43.

9. Hyde, DeLamater, Byers, *Understanding Human Sexuality*, Canadian edition (Toronto: McGraw-Hill, 2001), 683.

10. St. Stephen's Community House, *The Little Black Book: A Book on Healthy Sexuality Written by Grrrls For Grrrls* (Toronto: 2000), 152.

11. Karol E. Dean, Neil M. Malamuth, "Characteristics of Men Who Aggress Sexually and of Men Who Imagine Aggressing: Risk and Moderating Variables," *Journal of Personality and Social Psychology* 72 (1997), 449-455.

12. Karen Bouris, *The First Time: What Parents and Teenage Girls Should Know About "Losing Your Virginity"* (Berkeley, CA: Conari Press, 1994), 150.

13. Bouris, 154.

14. Maticka-Tyndale, 14.

15. *Teenage sexual and reproductive behavior in developed countries: Can more progress be made?* (Executive summary.) (New York: Alan Guttmacher Institute 2001), 2.

16. King, 144.

17. Robert A. Hatcher et al, *Contraceptive Technology,* 17th edition (New York: Arcent Media, 1998), 306.

18. John Guillebaud, *Contraception: Your Questions Answered,* third edition (Toronto: Churchill Livingstone, 1999), 42.

19. For more on microbicides see the article in *The Toronto Star,* June 3, 2000, A16.

20. Chart rates are based on information from *Contraceptive Technology* and *Understanding Human Sexuality.*

21. *The Little Black Book,* 74.

22. "Pregnant? Thinking About It?" Pamphlet from Ontario Ministry of Health, March 2002.

23. Bouris, 154.

24. Rochester STD/HIV Risk Reduction Training Centre, Monroe County, Department of Health, University of Rochester.

25. To quote Lyba Spring, sexual health educator for Toronto Public Health.

26. Rebecca Schleifer, "Ignorance Only: HIV/AIDS, Human Rights and Federally Funded Abstinence-Only Programs in the United States. Texas: A Case Study," *Human Rights Watch* 14, no. 5(G) (September 2002). Interview with Linda Grisham, teacher, Temple High School, Temple, Texas, May 6, 2002.

27. B. Risman and P. Schwartz, "Teen Sex after the Revolution: Gender Politics in Dating," *Context Magazine* (American Sociological Association), February 2000, 45.

28. Maticka-Tyndale, 9–11.

29. Anthony E. Wolf, *Get Out Of My Life But First Could You Drive Me and Cheryl to the Mall? A Parent's Guide to the New Teenager* (New York: The Noonday Press, 1991), 173–4.

30. Wolf, 176.

INDEX

CREDITS

"When are you fertile?" chart adapted and reprinted with the permission of Toronto Public Health. The poem "I Guess One Day" is reprinted with permission of St. Stephen's Community House from *The Little Black Book: A Book on Healthy Sexuality Written by Grrrls For Grrrls* (Toronto: 2000). Sexual positions photography by Trevor Stratton.

Illustrations and drawings pages 15, 31, 43, 50, 62, 78, 79, 92, 101, 102, 104, 118, 121, 139, 170, 181 Kim Smith. Illustrations and drawings pages 71, 91, 134, Kim Martyn. Illustrations pages 68, 99, 147, 166 Gelico.